W9-BLX-976

Bellow's People

ALSO BY DAVID MIKICS

Slow Reading in a Hurried Age

The Annotated Emerson

Who Was Jacques Derrida? An Intellectual Biography

A New Handbook of Literary Terms

WITH STEPHEN BURT

The Art of the Sonnet

Bellow's People

How Saul Bellow Made Life into Art

DAVID MIKICS

W. W. NORTON & COMPANY
INDEPENDENT PUBLISHERS SINCE 1923
NEW YORK | LONDON

Portions of *Bellow's People* have appeared, in different form, in *The Yale Review* (Spring 2014), *The Nation* (September 10, 2015), and *Tablet Magazine* (June 10, 2015).

Printed in the United States of America
First Edition

Manufacturing by Berryville Gaphics
Book design by Fearn Cutler de Vicq
Production manager: Julia Druskin

ISBN 978-0-393-24687-2

W. W. Norton & Company, Inc.
500 Fifth Avenue, New York, N.Y. 10110
www.wwnorton.com

W. W. Norton & Company Ltd.
Castle House, 75/76 Wells Street, London W1T 3QT

1 2 3 4 5 6 7 8 9 0

for Victoria and Ariel

CONTENTS

Bellow's People

INTRODUCTION

IN A PHOTO taken sometime in the late fifties, the sizing-up gaze from dark-pool eyes, the Buster Keaton–like, chiseled cheekbones (Bellow the schoolboy was nicknamed Buster), the knowing mouth with its gap tooth, the wide, ready lips. Happy strong and open, which makes us happy too, this face, but just maybe about to take some advantage. The face of someone who lives on talk, appetite, settling accounts, and writing, writing himself and writing other people.

"HE WAS GOING to take on more than the rest of us were," Alfred Kazin wrote about the young Saul Bellow, newly arrived in 1940s New York. "He was wary—eager, sardonic, and wary." Bellow, Kazin noted, was then not yet a novelist, much less a great one, but he had a pressing sense of his own coming destiny, "like an old Jew who feels himself closer to God than anybody else."

A hundred years after he was born, Bellow may seem to us a figure from the past, a vigorous old uncle in danger of being forgotten by readers. But we cannot let go of him, because he has lessons for us that we need to hear. Few novelists have ever given us such a wealth of high-wire verve, the excitement of funny, passionate, overwrought people seeking and squabbling and contending. Bellow's sentences live on the page, even burst from it. "Instantly we know whose words are loaded with life, and whose not," Emerson wrote. Bellow's lines are loaded, every one.

The first lesson Bellow teaches is attention to personality. Bellow is our novelist of personality in all its wrinkles, its glories and shortcomings. Only through personality, he tells us, can we know the world. Bellow writes people in a way that's rare among novelists. His universe is physical: people are their bodies and their faces, and their souls shine through their flesh. Take the actor Murphy Verviger in *Humboldt's Gift*, rehearsing at a Broadway theater that looks "like a gilded cake-platter with grimed frosting": "Verviger, his face deeply grooved at the mouth, was big and muscular. He resembled a skiing instructor. Some concept of intense refinement was eating at him. His head was shaped like a busby, a high solid arrogant rock covered with thick moss." Or Humboldt himself in his desperate last days: "He wore a large gray suit in which he was floundering. His face was dead gray, East River gray. His head looked as if the gypsy moth had gotten into it and tented in his hair." Every Bellow fan has a mental list of such gloriously precise human pictures. In each one, Bellow shows how the psyche is right there in the flesh, ready to be seen. In Bellow's descriptions, as James Wood comments, every detail is essential. He rivals even Dickens in his power to locate us through observation, to explain how appearances tell who we are.

Readers who love Bellow's books are sometimes a little embarrassed, as if Bellow caters to an indulgence, a mere taste for excitable people and hyped-up talk. Bellow fans fear they might be out for gossip rather than some more respectable nourishment. But there is no reason for embarrassment. In Bellow personality is an exalted thing, and the novels have a mood of restless discovery. Every face, every line of dialogue, can be a revelation.

Personality is different from cultural identity, though cultural identity helps to form and shape personality. Nation, tribe, sex, all are part of us. These identities, as Bellow understands them, are the product of real, sometimes brutal historical experience rather than any deliberate choice. Sammler, in *Mr. Sammler's Planet*, never chose to be a Jew in Nazi-occupied Europe. Chicago's poor urban blacks, in *The Dean's December*, didn't choose their particular misery either. When Sammler looks out on the sixties youth performing their hip ideal selves—guerrilla, long-haired cowboy, black panther—he sees something that we twenty-first-century readers recognize. We can make ourselves interesting, we think, by putting on a style, a stance, an identity: we are what we wear, how we look, what we buy, what we tweet. Bellow is here to tell us that this is all an empty fantasy. Personality is marked in every face we meet, long before we begin our social role-playing.

THIS BOOK IS CALLED *Bellow's People* because it describes some of the pungent, unforgettable personalities that Bellow knew and transformed in his books—his friends, family, wives, sworn enemies: Morrie Bellows, his eldest brother; Ralph Ellison (who barely shows up in Bellow's writing, but who influenced him greatly); Sondra Tschacbasov and Jack Ludwig, Bellow's wife and best friend, whose affair he fictionalized in *Herzog*; Chanler Chapman, Delmore Schwartz, and Allan Bloom, the originals of Bellow's Henderson, Humboldt, and Ravelstein; Alexandra Ionescu Tulcea Bellow, his wife during his late middle age; and two more best friends and intellectual influences, Isaac Rosenfeld and Edward Shils. Many more characters from Bellow's life appear in these pages. These men and women impelled him to become the writer he was.

Some accused Bellow of betraying the friends whose lives he used in his fiction. Joseph Epstein makes this charge in his portrait of the perfidious "Noah Danzig," which appeared in *Commentary* in 1990 ("Another Rare Visit with Noah Danzig"). Danzig is, transparently, Bellow. Danzig/Bellow, says Epstein, exploits the lives of others to make his ruthless art. He is only interested in people because they are fictional material. After mining their lives for his books, he discards them.

Epstein's Danzig has an "expansive, toothy smile," just like Bellow. As Epstein's attack gathers steam he displays a Bellow-like flair for portraying physiognomy, this time Bellow's own: "One of his front teeth was slightly longer than the other. And Gogol would have greatly enjoyed describing his thin, high-bridged nose with its large and dark nostrils, faintly quivering, as if taking the scent of something vaguely disgusting." That "great quivering, bony, black-holed nose," Epstein continues, "was dark red at its tip. It was nearly the same color as the maroon of his tie and matching socks. He was wearing a checked suit, with sharply cut lapels and small, high pockets cut into the trousers. The effect was lavish but somehow resembled the combination of a best man at a lower-middle-class wedding and a racetrack tout."

These withering lines are not a bad description of Bellow's characteristic natty attire. But they are crueler than anything Bellow himself ever wrote, which somewhat cuts the high ground out from under Epstein's feet. Epstein suggests that Bellow's point is to reduce people in his writing, to satirize them. Yet this is far from the truth. Somehow, magically, Bellow's own characters are never diminished to caricature but rendered more greatly themselves, even when Bellow pierces them through with his novelist's eye.

Epstein's case against Bellow is in part petty—Bellow insulted his friend Hilton Kramer in *Humboldt's Gift*, and Epstein's essay was a form of payback—but it is also quite serious. He writes, "When one went to hear Heifetz play

Beethoven, after all, it was more for the Heifetz than for the Beethoven. Similarly, one read a Danzig novel less for the normal pleasures of fiction than to watch Noah perform on the page."

Bellow is indeed a performing writer, but the people he depicts always share in the performance. I return more than a few times in this book to a comparison between Bellow and Nabokov, because Nabokov too is a performer, an enormously brilliant one. Nabokov, however, often works at the expense of his characters; Bellow works for them. As Joan Ullman, whose affair with the art critic Harold Rosenberg Bellow describes in his short story "What Kind of Day Did You Have," told me, "He brought Harold back." Elephantine flaws and all, Rosenberg was bigger than life, and Bellow proved it in his story (which was written after Rosenberg's death; the two men, longtime friends, both taught at the University of Chicago's Committee on Social Thought).

Bellow was a remarkable short story writer, one of the best of the twentieth century, but I've focused on his novels, where he had the large canvas he needed for his vision. I say little about his first two books, *Dangling Man* and *The Victim*, because Bellow himself regarded them as his apprentice work. Throughout I interweave vignettes of the people in Bellow's life with my sense of his books. Bellow wanted us to think about the real lives that he used in his work. Instead of simply exploiting the people he knew, as Epstein charged, Bellow, like Proust, was trying to understand them by turning them into fictions.

IN 1964 Bellow became an influential presence in America, a wealthy man and a famous one, through his novel *Herzog*, the best seller that introduced a distinctively Jewish overexcitement to the culture. The personality of Bellow's hero is what made the splash. Herzog teetered both intellectually and emotionally, exulting and then nearly breaking down. Comic and serious at once, never fragile or skittish, he was a vital, insightful wreck. His life was a mess he had made, but he had integrity too, and an odd dignity. He would have been at home in a Russian novel—perhaps Goncharov's *Oblomov* or Dostoevsky's *The Idiot*.

Bellow's Jewish hero Herzog hit a nerve. In *Herzog*'s wake came Bernard Malamud's *The Fixer*, Philip Roth's *Portnoy's Complaint*, and, of course, more books by Bellow. As Jonathan Liu comments in a review of *Witz*, Joshua Cohen's recent burlesque monument to the Jewish novel, in postwar American fiction Jews were the small slice of the population that came to represent the whole. Nervous stunts of self-definition, bold tightrope walking over pits of "self-alienation, historical dislocation, sexual neurosis, survivor's ambivalence": these traits, Liu remarks, proved basic to the postwar American novel, whether it was written by a Jew or not. In the decades after World War II, the fictional Jew let all that restrained WASP anxiety rise to the surface and made it burst open.

Jews also represented something "gravely universal," even "world-historical," Liu adds. Ancestry was destiny, and so American Jews carried a heavy double burden: they were connected to the Holocaust, the emblematic mass-scale barbarity of the twentieth century, and yet they had escaped that catastrophe, much as America itself had escaped the traumas of Europe.

For Bellow, who was born in a Yiddish-speaking home in Lachine, Quebec, Jewishness was simply a fact of life, something to be grateful for rather than to be puzzled over. Bellow was sent to heder at the age of four, where he began to learn Hebrew and, he said, "to memorize most of Genesis." He remarked late in his life that "it would be a treason to my first consciousness to un-Jew myself. One may be tempted to go behind the given and invent something better, to attempt to re-enter life at a more advantageous point. In America this is common, we have all seen it done, and done in many instances with great ingenuity. But the thought of such an attempt never entered my mind." Bellow was no new-made Gatsby: he was Jewish to the core, and spoke a fine Yiddish to his last days.

What does it mean to be a Jew? Am I really a Jew? Am I too much a Jew, or too little?—these questions, so basic to Bellow's younger rival, Philip Roth, never appear in Bellow's writing. Roth was the herald of the new identity game; he made Gatsby-like self-invention the essence of Jewishness. For Bellow, by contrast, a Jew was a Jew, just as an American was an American. Bellow's confidence about Jewishness belongs to an earlier era, but it has much to teach us: sometimes being a Jew is a simple fact, rather than, as in Roth and Bernard Malamud, an agonized one.

In the mid-sixties Bellow edited a book titled *Great*

Jewish Short Stories. In the introduction, he wrote, "I would call the attitudes of these stories characteristically Jewish. In them, laughter and trembling are so curiously mingled that it is not easy to determine the relations of the two. . . . At times the figures of the story, or parable, appear to invite or encourage trembling with the secret aim of overcoming it by means of laughter."

This is a radically different idea of Jewishness in literature from the social-identity idea voiced by the critic Leslie Fiedler, in a famous 1949 essay in *Commentary* entitled "What Can We Do About Fagin?" Fiedler issued a call to arms. He wanted to counteract the bad images of "the Jew" in English and American literature; he called for new, positive myths of Jewishness. Later that year *Commentary* printed responses to Fiedler by, among others, Harold Rosenberg, Stanley Edgar Hyman, Philip Rahv, Harry Levin, Irving Howe, Alfred Kazin, Lionel Trilling—and Bellow. Bellow's answer to Fiedler was, in essence, that literature is not PR: there is no point in wrangling over stereotypes, and especially not in order to make new stereotypes. Creating praiseworthy images may be the task of socialist realism, but it is not real exploration. We need to dig deeper, Bellow implied, to discover what the word "Jewish" might mean.

For the routine nostalgic decorations that are thought to make a novel "Jewish," Bellow in his introduction to *Great Jewish Short Stories* has nothing but disdain. He dismisses "prayer shawls and phylacteries and Sabbath sentiment, the Seder, the matchmaking, the marriage canopy; for sadness the Kaddish, for amusement the *schnorrer*, for admiration the bearded scholar." Bellow goes at Jewishness free-style, his own way; the myths that comfort others have no appeal for him. But he doesn't want a bold new image either, unless it's the reality he knows best, the ravenous Jewish intellectuals he lives among.

BELLOW IS a natural comedian, and so his piece on Jewish short story writers becomes an argument for the depth of their comedy. Clearly, he is thinking of his own work too when he writes, "The real secret, the ultimate mystery, may never reveal itself to the earnest thought of a Spinoza, but when we laugh (the idea is remotely *Hasidic*) our minds refer us to God's existence. Chaos is *exposed*." With his practice of serious comedy in his books, Bellow makes us think not just of Jewish authors like Sholem Aleichem or Isaac Babel, but of Dostoevsky, with his frantic, hugely entertaining sufferers.

Bellow is one of the most personal and intimate of fiction writers. What he values most of all is the battered heart, and its dealings with the world. Yet his work is not at all grim: he might be the funniest of our major writers. "'I have suffered,' he said, and then he laughed as if nothing could be funnier": so Susan Cheever in one of her memoirs remembers Bellow at a party. He tells us something that cannot be told by the intellectual, the editorialist, the historian, or the political commentator—something that sparks the soul, and wants to wake it up.

"Things around Saul were magical," Leon Wieseltier

told me. "He noticed more so I noticed more. The vitality was off the charts; it was physical, it was intellectual. The thing that offended Saul more than anything was drowsiness." Wakefulness was Bellow's constant goal, Wieseltier said. "He lived in the present in a ferocious way. The New York intellectuals were always looking for masters who weren't themselves. Saul didn't do that. There was something so deeply unsubservient about Saul. His mind was as good as anybody's mind, he thought. He didn't have reverence. He blew the whole thing up, even though he was one of them. He gave you this feeling of being primary, which is a very rare feeling."

Bellow is sometimes called a novelist of ideas, but he sensed that ideas can block life. His particular target was the New York intellectuals, the gang he ran with but also the frequent object of his attacks. In a letter to Fiedler in June 1955, he wrote, "I don't consider myself part of the *Partisan* group. Not those dying beasts." He delighted in introducing the eminences of *Partisan Review* to Dave Peltz, a colorful and louche pal whom he'd known since he was a teenager. He assigned Peltz to show Hannah Arendt around Chicago when she was considering a job at the university (in the end, the meeting between Peltz and Arendt never took place). Once Bellow and Peltz took Lionel Trilling slumming after a lecture, standing him drinks in a dive bar. "A cold coming we had of it," Bellow joked in a letter, likening these three diverse Jews to T. S. Eliot's Magi.

The intellectual's doom occurs when he chooses ideas over the lively world. In *Humboldt's Gift*, Bellow reluctantly judges that the madcap and mad Von Humboldt Fleisher, based on his friend Delmore Schwartz, has succumbed to ideas. He has made himself boring, and so turned his back on life. "Humboldt had become boring in the vesture of a superior person, in the style of high culture, with all of his conforming abstractions. Many hundreds of thousands of people were now wearing this costume of the higher misery." Bellow's task is to shake us out of this straitjacket, the higher misery of ideas. Yet he loved ideas, too: you had to go through them to get out of them. His son Adam recalled that Bellow "once told me that he'd worked through all the ideologies of the twentieth century so that I wouldn't have to. I still did, though."

A little-noticed article that Bellow wrote for *Encounter* in 1963, "Some Notes on Recent American Fiction," is his declaration of independence as a writer, or at least the place where he declared what he wasn't. He wrote the essay as he was finishing *Herzog*, and it shows: his tacit job is to figure out how this book, in which Bellow truly comes into his own, outdoes its rivals. American fiction seems narrow to Bellow, which makes him ask some old-new questions: What can a novel tell us about ourselves? And what has the self become anyway in the twentieth century?

In his *Encounter* essay Bellow rejects what he calls the writers of "sensibility," the craftsmen (and women) of inwardness. He remarks, "The individual in American fiction often comes through to us, especially among writers of 'sensibility,' as a colonist who has been sent to a remote place, some Alaska of the soul. What he has to bring under cultivation, however, is a barren emptiness within himself."

Bellow's chief example of sensibility is John Updike, who would become a long-running critical foe, a habitual negative reviewer of Bellow's books in *The New Yorker*. What Updike's self-cultivation really amounts to, Bellow says, is "the rearrangement of things in new and hostile solitude." About Updike's story "Pigeon Feathers" Bellow remarks cuttingly, "We suspect [sensibility] of a stony heart because it functions so smoothly in its isolation." And the "stoicism of separateness" in Hemingway or John O'Hara also seems arid to Bellow, much like Updike's method. Like the writer of sensibility, the stoic is an obsessive craftsman. Bellow wants something wider and freer.

Bellow showed an intense concern with *Lolita* in his 1963 *Encounter* essay. Nabokov's scandalous tour de force had taken the literary world by storm with its American publication five years earlier; *Herzog* would achieve a similar victory. But Bellow was determined to make *Herzog* a far different book from *Lolita*. Bellow compares *Lolita* to *Death in Venice* and is troubled by the decline of desire from Mann to Nabokov. Mann's "sad occurrence involves Apollo and Dionysus," he writes, whereas "the internal life of Humbert Humbert has become a joke." Humbert "is a fourth- or fifth-rate man of the world and is unable to be entirely serious about his passion." Bellow adds, "The earnestness of Mann about love and death might be centuries old. The same subject is sadly and maliciously comical in *Lolita*."

Nabokov's Quilty doesn't take his own death seriously, and so loses "a life that was not worth having anyway."

Nabokov, of course, poked fun at what he considered Mann's plaster-of-paris pretense to great themes and ideas; his ironies were more corrosive, and also easier, than Mann's. But the Nabokovian magician's hat looked to Bellow disturbingly like an empty vessel. Bellow was never interested in the solemn Old World pacing that Mann perfected, the languor and the *Abendland* mood, but he was not one of Nabokov's game players either. The sensitive inwardness of an Updike and the hard-boiled stoic stance he had already rejected. What was left was Bellow's own pathway, the one he carved out most memorably in *Herzog*: a comic seriousness, an overspilling desperate gusto, the crazy turmoil of a life.

Comedy like Nabokov's, Bellow knew, likes to lacerate the staid and bourgeois, but the artistic types don't come off much better. Humbert hilariously explodes respectable Charlotte Haze, but Humbert himself is a shabby rather than a gay monster. There is no one to champion, unless it be the defensive and somber married Lolita, seen briefly after her escape from Humbert: but she is only glimpsed, not allowed to influence the later course of the story, which is governed by Quilty's and Humbert's restless antics. Bellow's unspoken question in his essay, fully embodied in *Herzog*, is: How can comedy build something up, rather than just being a way to knock the self down? As Bellow saw it, in his books before *Herzog* he had not truly reached the soul. He had been exuberant, in *The Adventures of Augie March* and

Henderson the Rain King. He had been intense, even dire, in *Seize the Day* and his first two novels. But his work fell into these two halves—it was either freewheeling or deliberately confined—and therefore the work was incomplete. With *Herzog* Bellow would break through, complete himself, and readers realized the difference right away.

In his novels Bellow refuses most of the usual themes of fiction: there's no Julien Sorel–like remaking of identity, and no puzzles of inwardness to solve, as with James or Tolstoy, who make us try to figure out who their characters really are (James does it teasingly, Tolstoy satisfyingly). Bellow's characters are who they are from the beginning; they seldom grow or decline. In Bellow personality is performance, and its way is basically comic: self-delighting, unfolded all at once.

Bellow's comedy is, like all the best comedy, neither too naïve nor too knowing, and so it takes a stand against irony, which always knows too much. Irony is the novel's achievement but also, as Bellow recognizes, its danger. Stendhal and Flaubert pioneered novelistic irony: they lovingly absorbed romantic idealism in their work but corrected it with a dose of cynicism, and by doing so suggested that romanticism was nothing so special, but rather common currency. Ever since these two French titans wrote, some major novelists have, in the name of realism, deliberately—ironically—allowed the way the culture talks and thinks to infect their style. For Joyce, realism meant being able to take seriously the cheapest clichés about love and success, and even to give new life to these clichés. But Joyce retained the ironist's privilege: he looked down on the popular speech that he also caressed. The privilege was handed down to Nabokov, Pynchon, David Foster Wallace. An alternative was to achieve something purer and sparer than the popular dialects that swirl around the writer, and this way of writing has flourished too, from Kafka and Camus to Marilynne Robinson.

Bellow sounds nothing like any of the authors I have just mentioned. His style is an original creation, fully colloquial but all his own. It is wrought from Yiddish as well as English and is just as precise as it is headlong. Bellow stirs in the pot some minor touches of eighteenth-century archaism, too. Consider a sentence from *Augie March* (the character Mimi has just endured a back-alley abortion): "She bled very swift, and she tried to keep it secret, but presently she had to tell me, as she herself, astonished, tried to keep track of it." Note the choice of "swift" rather than "quickly," and the faint starch of "presently": the sentence would be at home in Fielding.

Yiddish syntax and rhythm animate Bellow, but quietly, so that a reader unfamiliar with Yiddish will hardly sense its presence. Here is a monumental sentence from, again, *Augie March*. Bellow is describing that Armenian supermaven, Mintouchian: "He had legs on him like that statue of Clemenceau on the Champs Elysées where Clemenceau is striding against a wind and is thinking of bread and war, and the misery and grandeur, going on with last strength in his longjohns and gaiters." The slangy "he had legs on him" and the "a" in "against a wind" surely come from Yiddish.

How perfect the "the" before "misery," also a Yiddishism! Add or subtract a "the" from the string of nouns (bread, war, misery, grandeur) and the rhythm of the sentence would collapse. "Erratic is nothing," says Mintouchian to Augie: just behind these words lurks the Yiddish *iz gornisht*. Bellow did with Yiddish what Ellison did with African American English: he let it inflect his writing subtly, pervasively. To call Bellow a great stylist is the kiss-off of death, too faint a compliment. Instead, style tells who he is, and, in his books, who everybody is.

Bellow himself was a man of style, well put together in dress and speech and gleaming with wit. Thankfully, though, he stayed rough, not polished; he was tousled both emotionally and intellectually. "He reminded many people of their incompleteness, perhaps because he knew of his own," writes Edward Rothstein, who was one of Bellow's students at Chicago, in a *New York Times* article: "There was a rawness to him, almost like a wound, underneath the genteel polish and fiendish wit. His feathered fedora and striped shirts, his elegant manners and silken voice were enameled surfaces, under which he was, like his characters, at sea, the imposing intellect unable to ever lay down any reliable anchor—and not for want of trying, not for want of greatness."

The man or woman of style aims at a never possible completeness. But style conceals, too: beneath it are the raw, unhealed emotions that Bellow knew well. Bellow in his work and life went for incomplete people, because he knew he was one of them.

BELLOW'S INTIMATELY FAST-PACED, thought-ruffled, and emotionally cadenced prose style from *Augie March* on was his way of getting close to the culture of the Jewish America he knew, talk-addled as it was and intoxicated with words. "At a most susceptible time of my life I was wholly Jewish," Bellow once told an interviewer. "That's a gift, a piece of good fortune with which one does not quarrel." He meant his childhood in Montreal and, later, Chicago: the cramped, dingy heder; the march through *aleph-beys* and Torah; the treasures of his native language, Yiddish; and the range of Jewish personalities that populate his work. In a late-in-life interview with Norman Manea, the Romanian writer, Bellow remembered that when he was a small boy in Montreal "I went across the street to Shikka Stein," the *melamed* who instructed the boys, "and he taught me my Alef-Beis and then we began to read Breishis [Genesis] and then we began to read Rashi and it was wonderful. . . . I was four years old and my head was in a spin. I would come out of Shikka Stein's apartment and sit on the curb and think it all over in front of my house." In his eighties Bellow was still thinking it over: he told Manea that every day he read in Hebrew a bit of Genesis or Exodus or the books of Samuel.

Near the end of his life, then, Bellow returned to reading the Hebrew scriptures he had first seen at age four. The older he got, the more he liked to speak Yiddish, the language his parents used with him. Jews, Bellow suggested, seem to know something that many other Americans don't: you can't really make yourself over, and so you remain bound to your earliest attachments. Bellow honors this first Jewish knowledge, with its undodgeable family ties, in his fine short story "The Old System."

Bellow's Jews stood in contrast to the much more anxious and constricted ones so artfully described by Bernard Malamud, just a year older and from a similar hardworking family. Bellow also differed from the shrewdly conniving fable-maker Isaac Bashevis Singer, whose story "Gimpel the Fool" Bellow translated in 1952, introducing Singer's work to an English-speaking audience. Bellow improvised his lively translation of "Gimpel" in a few hours while Eliezer Greenberg read the story aloud in Yiddish. Bellow translated off the cuff and Irving Howe watched, he said, "in a state of high excitement" ("It was a feat of virtuosity, and we drank a schnapps to celebrate," Howe added). But the hard edge of Singer's story was foreign to Bellow, who trusted human desire in a way that Singer, who lived in a world ruled by demons of perversity and frustration, refused to do.

Bellow's translation of "Gimpel" is a marvel: a few times he sounds more Yiddish than the original. Take Singer's sentence *Az Got git pleytzes muz men shlepn dem pak* ("since God gives shoulders, you have to carry the pack"), which Bellow turns into this: "Shoulders are from God, and burdens too." Singer resented Bellow for never translating another of his stories, and the relationship between the two writers did not flourish. Bellow later described himself as a collector of anecdotes about Singer's abundant bad behavior.

The much younger Philip Roth was both closer to and further away from Bellow than any other Jewish novelist. Bellow strongly defended Roth's controversial *Goodbye, Columbus* in a 1959 *Commentary* review, but combined his praise with a warning against wry sophistication. "Sometimes he twinkles too much," Bellow wrote about Roth. Bellow sensed that Roth was out to make a statement about the material abundance of Jewish life in America. "Nothing like it has ever hit the world," Bellow acknowledges, but it's clear that he himself has no interest in sociological description—he doesn't care what's in the Patimkins' refrigerator. Roth, who will be so taken up with the argument between the demands of artistic vocation and fleshly desire, differs enormously from Bellow. Both were conscious of the artistic qualities that separated them. Roth's portrait of Bellow as the distinguished showman-like Jewish writer Felix Abravanel in *The Ghost Writer*, written in 1979, makes Bellow look like a lightweight next to his Malamud figure, Lonoff, the idolized central character of Roth's novel and a saintly though crotchety expert in self-denial.

Bellow was deeply stung by the way Roth turned him into Abravanel, a proud dandy in a finely tailored suit whose "charm was like a moat so oceanic that you could not even see the great turreted and buttressed thing it had been dug to protect." Abravanel is aloof, defensive, supremely guarded, and, Roth's narrator remembers, he "seemed to prefer to look down at us from a long way off, like a llama or a camel." Interestingly, Roth makes Abravanel a tall man, unlike the bantam-size Bellow. Roth himself is tall, and there is a bit of Abravanel in him, too—Roth has his own charm moat. But Roth was no doubt also alluding to the fact that so many of Bellow's heroes are men of great height, even the ones clearly based on Bellow himself: Herzog, Citrine.

"I loved the depiction of Saul as Abravanel," Bellow's son Adam told me, but Bellow himself was offended. Roth and Bellow eventually patched up their friendship, but the damage had been done. Bellow's sense of injury reverberated for some time: "What hath Roth got?" Bellow once asked on *The Dick Cavett Show.* Roth dedicated his book *Reading Myself and Others* to Bellow, but in it he expressed reservations about Bellow's novels. Late in their lives, Roth and Bellow largely resolved their differences, and Roth was a frequent visitor to Bellow's home in Vermont.

In his Nobel lecture in 1976, Bellow lamented the avalanche of high ideas that buried writers in the twentieth century. Such ideas, he said, had become nothing better than received opinions, preventing us from seeing what we really are, which is, as Bellow never tired of asserting, the one true task of the novelist. Bellow declared in his Nobel lecture that

> essay after essay, book after book, confirms the most serious thoughts—Baudelairean, Nietzschean, Marxian, psychoanalytic, et cetera, et cetera . . . maintaining all the usual things about mass society, dehumanization and the rest. How poorly they represent us. The pictures they offer no more resemble

> us than we resemble the reconstructed reptiles and other monsters in a museum of paleontology. We are much more limber, versatile, better articulated, there is much more to us—we all feel it.

Bellow in his long life of writing did the most he could to confirm our feeling that there is much more to us than our Horatios, the men and women who swear by ideas, can ever show. "The essence of our real condition," he announced in Stockholm, "the complexity, the confusion, the real pain of it, is shown to us in glimpses, in what Proust and Tolstoy thought of as 'true impressions.'"

Novelists can glean such impressions only if they stop thinking of people from a distance. Bellow calls on writers to reject the revolution led by Flaubert, which elevated the artist-creator above the world he set out to depict. Instead, novelists must remain true to the origin of all novels: the people they know, the real-life characters who get turned into fiction.

Bellow well knew that such truth-bound realism often enough requires the writer to betray real people in order to remake them, so they can join a fictional world that resembles as nearly as possible the one we know. As much as Proust or Tolstoy, Bellow was a student of betrayal in his work, and he himself betrayed wives and friends. But he was also loyal to who they were, determined to see them totally, to know them and make them live in his work. Herzog's Madeleine was not Bellow's ex-wife Sondra Tschacbasov, as Tschacbasov herself declared: the fictional

Madeleine was pure in her rage, a work of tempestuous art, never doubtful or wavering like the actual Sondra. Nor was Bellow himself Herzog. But we are right to be confused about this question of life and art in Bellow, since the confusion is so rewarding. The tangled lines that run between lived experience and the novelist's reworking of life are unusually rich and dense and telling in Bellow. The more we return to Bellow's actual people, the more we learn about the characters they became—and usually, stunningly, the reverse is true too. Can anyone who knew Allan Bloom remember him without also remembering Bellow's Ravelstein? Delmore Schwartz is now, at least in large part, Von Humboldt Fleisher.

Bellow took liberties in his writing. Anger, not just affection, washes across his refashioning of lived fact into fictions. He was constantly involved, compromised; his quest was always a personal one. In this way he stayed true to what he saw as the novelist's highest purpose: to make the people he had known and loved even more real, and more lasting.

CHAPTER I

Morrie Bellows

SOLOMON (SHLOIMKE) BELLOW, later Saul, was born in Quebec in 1915 and smuggled nine years later under the unwatchful eyes of border police to dark, immigrant-packed, blustery Chicago. Bellow's father, Abraham, who had escaped from prison in czarist Russia, was a bootlegger, a baker, and, later, a coalyard owner. Solomon, the youngest child of Abraham and his wife, Liza Gordon, had three older siblings, Jane, Maurice (called Morrie or Maury), and Sam. His brothers became businessmen, and both later changed their last name to Bellows, just as Bellow renamed himself Saul. The eldest brother, Morrie, was a hard, echt Chicago get-ahead man who boasted about money and slapped the shoulders of famous gangsters. Bellow, by contrast, early on sensed his readiness for a cash-poor writer's career, and was much mocked by Morrie on account of his teenage cultural pretensions.

While Morrie, seven years older, was working for a

living, young Solomon spent his free days at the public library reading Theodore Dreiser and Sherwood Anderson, and considering ways that a Jewish boy who spoke Yiddish, English, and French, who played stickball and kick-the-can in the streets of Humboldt Park (a Jewish enclave), might compare with these two working-class masters of American letters. Bellow especially loved Dreiser. He valued the way Dreiser put his arms around his characters, was so eager to accept and understand them, no matter how ragged or common their desires. But he recognized that Dreiser's style was flawed: at once too crude and too dressed up, full of strokes of fate and wooden editorializing. Above all, Dreiser was a tragic writer; Bellow wanted to go comic.

On a bitter cold morning in 1938, the twenty-three-year-old Bellow started out for his first day of work in Morrie's coalyard. A recent dropout from his anthropology master's program at the University of Wisconsin, Bellow had just come back to Chicago and had gotten married to a local girl, Anita Goshkin. Morrie, who surfaces in *Augie March* as Augie's rage-filled, sneering older brother, often quarreled with Bellow. Morrie was adamantly a money Jew rather than a culture Jew. Alone among the Bellow family, Morrie refused to attend Saul's Nobel Prize ceremony in Stockholm. (Bellow later complained that his sister, Jane, fell asleep during his acceptance speech, but at least she made the trip.) He was to Bellow the ultimate reality instructor (a favorite term in Bellow): hard and unforgiving, an enemy of imagination.

Bellow's father, Abraham, was, like Morrie, a harsh reality instructor: for Abraham, life was business. In a 1937 letter to his high school friend Oscar Tarcov, Bellow wrote,

> My father, spongy soul, cannot give freely. His business conscience pursues him into private life. . . . He started giving me a Polonius, berating all my friends, warning me, adjuring me, doing everything short of damning me. . . . I blew up and told him precisely the place he occupied in my category of character, what I thought of his advice, and that I intended to live as I saw fit. . . . The coalbins resounded with my shouts and imprecations.

Bellow said to Tarcov that his father "boasts of having read the complete works of Pushkin, Lermontov, Chekhov, Tolstoi, Turgenev, and Dostoievsky. I believe him. But how has he been able to look open eyed at these men and act as he has shown himself capable of acting[?]"

Bellow was quickly fired from Morrie's coalyard for absenteeism. A few years earlier, in 1934, Morrie had fired him for reading on the job. There was to be no pact between the demands of art and those of the hardscrabble companies run by Abraham and his firstborn son, Morrie. Abraham also passed on his fierce anger to Morrie: both father and son were at war against the world.

"FUCK MORRIE. I only met Morrie once. What kind of family [member] is that?" Adam Bellow, Bellow's second son, said to me about his uncle. Morrie with his rages, his touchy arrogance, stood at the beginning and end of Saul's angry ambition as a writer. "He wanted to show Morrie," Adam remarked. "'Revenge is a perfectly good motive for a writer to have,' he once said. You know, he just didn't go in for the whole Parnassian thing—it was all there, high and low; the low was the self too." Daniel Bellow told me that, like his brother Adam, he met Morrie just once. "He terrified me; he scared the living daylights out of me. He was a brilliant man in his way: his business head. Janis [Bellow's widow] said Pop's last words were 'I showed them'"—"them" being his father and Morrie. Daniel added, "Morrie was even more Pop's father than his father."

Morrie was his father's son. The fury that impelled Abraham also fired Morrie's restless moneymaking ambition. Near the beginning of his magisterial biography of Bellow, Zachary Leader describes a crucial moment in the family life of the Bellows in Montreal. In 1923 Abraham was badly in debt and desperately trying to make a living as a bootlegger. Abraham and his partner decided to go for broke. They borrowed some money and loaded up a rented truck with whiskey, ready to make a big sale to some gangsters from New York who would meet them when they crossed the border. But they never made it: somewhere near Montreal the truck was hijacked and stolen, along with the bootleg whiskey. The hijackers beat up Abraham and threw him in a ditch. Abraham climbed out of the ditch and started home on foot. The next morning Abraham's wife, Liza, sent out fifteen-year-old Morrie to find his father. As Leader tells the story, Morrie

> ran to the partner's place of work and waited. Eventually, he saw a figure in the distance, running "like the demons of hell were following him." It was his father, in torn clothes, bloody, in tears. Reaching out to him, the boy said, "Pa, Pa! What's wrong?" In the version of the story told by Maury's [Morrie's] son, "then my grandfather just beat the shit out of my father."

In *Herzog* Bellow tames the anecdote by leaving out the father's beating of his son.

Abraham's hot temper bore down on Morrie, who was almost always, as in the bootlegging anecdote, the first target of his father's wrath. Bellow once described his father in a letter as "a furious man, whirling with impatience . . . a heavyweight tyrant." Abraham Bellow was a man of passion, a volatile troublemaker who even in his sixties would sometimes get into street scraps. Changeable like a Dostoevsky character, Leader remarks, he could melt with emotion too. Bellow remembered that Abraham would read Sholem Aleichem to the family in the evenings, and he liked to watch the antics of his children.

Morrie was even more volatile than Abraham. Pa should have slapped you around like he did me, he liked to tell

Saul, it might have wised you up. Morrie took pride in his know-how, his connections. "Enough of this crap about being Jewish," he would say (unlike his brother Sam, who married a rabbi's daughter, Morrie early on stopped observing dietary laws). But Morrie's toughness went along with a vulnerability that was with him from childhood on. Morrie was a greedy, overweight child, Bellow remembered; the first son bore the brunt of his father's anger and survived by trying to amuse Abraham. Bellow wrote to his third wife, Susan Glassman, in 1962, that Morrie "freezes when he's offended, and if you think *I'm* vulnerable, I recommend you study him."

When Bellow was in third grade, Morrie was already a student at Tuley High School. Along with Sam, three years his younger, Morrie sold chocolate bars on the L and newspapers on the street. He was also a "baggage-smasher," heaving luggage onto trucks for American Express. He enrolled at a downtown law school, what Sandor Himmelstein in *Herzog* calls a "kike college," but never finished. Instead Morrie worked for one of Al Capone's lawyers collecting graft payments. Eventually he took over Abraham's coalyard, and then became a real estate tycoon, cutting a substantial figure in Chicago life. Sam also made money in Chicago real estate—he owned a chain of nursing homes—but his profile was much lower than his brother's.

After Morrie and his wife bought the Shoreland Hotel on the South Side, where Al Capone had done his business, it became a Teamsters headquarters. Jimmy Hoffa, who came to the wedding of Morrie's daughter, kept an apartment there, as did the economist Milton Friedman. In 1956, in front of the Shoreland, Morrie was nearly strangled by a Teamster whom he had unwisely challenged over an outstanding bill; the incident made the papers. In his retelling of the event in the short story "Cousins," Bellow remembered that the Teamster's Cadillac had a clergy sticker for parking purposes.

"He liked to abuse waiters, I saw him do it," Greg, Bellow's eldest son, said of his uncle Morrie. "He loved to lord it over people." Morrie regularly hit his children Joel and Lynn, just as Abraham had hit him. He was a man of appetite, an overeater his whole life; he owned three hundred suits and a hundred pairs of shoes. When Morrie visited Saul he would play the buffoon, pulling a book off the shelf and demanding, "Who's this guy Prowst?" (Ulick, the Morrie character in *Humboldt's Gift*, shuts himself in his office where he eats fistfuls of raisins and reads Cecil Roth and Salo Baron on Jewish history, but whenever high culture names come up in conversation, he makes sure to mispronounce them.) Once, when Bellow and his first wife were struggling to pay the bills, Morrie came to visit and hurled down a pile of his old shirts for his brother; this happens too in *Augie*, where Morrie plays a crucial role as Augie's brother Simon.

Morrie's most spectacular scandal stemmed from his affair with Marcie Borok, a nightclub dancer. In 1947 Marcie gave birth to a son, Dean, and then another son two years later (the second boy was not in fact Morrie's son, but another man's). Morrie, Marcie claimed, was the father and had agreed to adopt both children, but then changed his mind. She pursued Morrie to Miami, where he was staying with his wife, Marge, in the Saxony Hotel, partly owned by the Bellowses. Then the scandal broke: in December 1949 the *Miami Herald* ran a story headlined "Blonde Serves Club Owner as Father of Her Children." Marcie was only twenty, Morrie forty-one in 1949, when Marcie took Morrie to court. She may have also run after him with a loaded gun and even fired some shots at him, though the facts of the case remain in dispute.

In 1980 Dean Borok, who was living in Canada, read *Augie March* and discovered it contained a version of his mother's affair with Morrie. Borok began writing to Bellow, and Bellow wrote back at least once. Bellow said to Dean Borok about Morrie,

> He sees none of us—brothers, sister, or his two children—neither does he telephone or write. He had no need of us. He has no past, no history. . . . I tell you all this to warn you about the genes you seem so proud of. If you've inherited them (it's possible you have) many of them will have to be subdued or lived down. I myself have had some hard going with them.

Morrie met his son Dean Borok, chatted brusquely, and gave him money, but that was the end of it.

Borok is the spitting image of a Bellow, at least judging from the photos on his website. Not only his looks but his larger-than-life temper testify that he is Morrie's son. Borok kept writing to Bellow for over twenty years, and the letters, as Leader describes them, are vituperative, funny, and disturbing. Leader reports that in 1992 Borok sent Bellow two photos of himself, one in a tuxedo and another in a Speedo, along with a note saying, "You *never* looked this good." Borok ran an S-and-M leather store in Montreal and later became a stand-up comedian in New York. Bellow kept his letters. Brim-full of adrenaline and resentment, hacking away at Saul and Morrie alike, Borok might have been auditioning for a part in a Bellow novel. Leader's description calls to mind the savage, preening Cantabile in *Humboldt's Gift*, a handsome, cracked, testosterone-fueled goon, vindictive, exuberant, and unstoppable. Dean was a wild shard chipped from Morrie's block.

As Dean Borok discovered when he read *Augie March*, the novel contains a full, bruising, but also admiring portrait of his father, Morrie. Augie's brother Simon is a bully and adulterer, crass and aspiring. He coldly marries for money, not love, and he violently derides Augie's feckless nature, just as the unforgiving Morrie scorned Saul's lack of business acumen. Simon gives off a whiff of the unstable macho, the potent crazy: at one point he rips the cheap dress of his mother-in-law, telling her that she has embarrassed herself by wearing rags, with all her money. The mother-in-law, laughing appreciatively, forgives him. But the incident reveals a disquieting brutality in Simon.

There was more than a trace of Simon's—that is, Morrie's—passionate and reckless traits in the young

Bellow. Dave Peltz remembered the teenage Saul's jealous rage over his high school girlfriend Eleanor Fox. Once Bellow hitchhiked to Fox's summer house in Indiana, burst in, saw her wearing another boy's frat pin, and ripped it off. Naomi Lutz, the Eleanor character in *Humboldt's Gift*, reminds the grown-up Charlie Citrine of his uncontrollable jealousy. But the mild Augie completely lacks such off-kilter emotions; instead his brother Simon is the dress-tearing, mouth-foaming man of passion. In *Augie March* only Simon displays ominous masculine aggression. *Augie*'s gallery of tomcats is extensive, but except for Simon they are all charming rather than frightening.

Simon siphoned off all the anger that Bellow felt and feared in himself. In *Dangling Man* and *The Victim*, his first two books, the long-suffering heroes' rages are shameful, sudden, and unexpected. But Augie, like Henderson, doesn't have a truly angry bone in his body. Not until *Herzog* would Bellow dare to put his own sheer rage into his books and recognize his true kinship with Morrie.

The sadness of *Augie*'s portrait of Simon is clearly Bellow's own sadness toward Morrie: he displays a loving younger sibling's deeply disappointed judgment. But he also makes a case for Simon, as Leader remarks. He makes Morrie's anger seem vital rather than ruinous. In *Augie* Bellow remade his brother into a rough apostle of life, in place of the thwarted ogre that Morrie actually was.

While he was writing *Augie March* Bellow wrote to the editor Monroe Engel that the final section of *Augie* was going to be "a final, tragic one on the life of the greatest

Machiavellian of them all, Augie's brother Simon." But the book doesn't end this way. Simon is not a tragic figure, and neither was Morrie. Bellow's rash, violent eldest brother was no Dreiser hero. He was not shadowed by ruin; with no past at his back, he just threw off any misfortunes. Remarried and living in Thomasville, Georgia, Morrie gave no signs of being haunted by grief.

"He overpowered me and in a sense he led me to write *The Adventures of Augie March*," Bellow remarked about Morrie in an interview with Philip Roth. Was Morrie an intriguing Machiavellian or was he what Bellow's second wife, Sondra, called him, "a big fat pig of a vulgar man"? He was, of course, both: his strenuously willed ignorance, the way he swatted down culture and ideas, made him the Chicago man of power he wanted to be.

Simon tells Augie about Renee, who is transparently Marcie Borok. "Smiling," Simon says, "'She left her husband the same night we met. It was at a night club in Detroit. . . . I said, "Come along," and she's been with me ever since.'"

Augie says, "I was fascinated by him, by them both." But the line rings a little hollow. Augie's unruffled, calmly interested stance toward his brother is really Bellow's fantasy of keeping his distance from the turbulent Morrie.

Bellow started thinking about power under the influence of anxious, overbearing Morrie. But *Augie March* was a way of freeing himself from Morrie's influence: Bellow planted Augie's own happy-go-lucky instinct for freedom in the center of his book. By coloring Simon with some of

Augie's own vitality, his fresh aptitude for more life, Bellow redeemed his brother. This is true of the book's other males on the prowl too. The powerful men in *Augie March* are winning rather than dangerous, from the clumsy Five Properties to the lustful, flirtatious William Einhorn; Einhorn's father, the roosterish Commissioner; and his goofball half brother, the perfectly named Dingbat.

Bellow commented once that the most memorable character in *The Brothers Karamazov* was not Ivan or the saintly Alyosha, but their father, old man Karamazov, that repulsive yet entrancing buffoon. "The boldest comedians are the ones who, like Old Karamazov, have revised all social and traditional fictions in the clear light of first principles as *they* see them," Bellow insisted. Bellow turns wild, brutal Fyodor Karamazov into the true hero of Dostoevsky's great novel in part because the old man resembles in his reckless éclat his own father, Abraham, and his elder brother Morrie. On a diminished scale, the Bellows echo the most renowned family in the novel's history, with Bellow himself as the turbulent, doubt-daring Ivan, and his brother Sam as the strong and wholesome Alyosha.

Bellow also names Fyodor his favorite because the Karamazovs' father is a pure hero of personality. The most embarrassing father in literature, far outstripping King Lear, Fyodor Pavlovich Karamazov is cunning, silly, perverse, pretending always to be stupidly sure of himself, mocking fancy ideas, and hating the respectable more than anything. Like the rough Chicago types Bellow knew from childhood on, old Karamazov barges ahead, a ham actor and man of appetite.

Bellow's own self-confidence was far more canny, more controlled, than that of a reckless Karamazov, or of Morrie with his battering-ram *macher*'s will. Dave Peltz said about the future novelist, "He was focused, he was dedicated to becoming what he was, from the beginning. I mean he never veered. He believed in himself." Morrie was just as implacable, but unlike Bellow he wanted to get rid of the past, the childhood memories that were for Bellow the core of his being. Thirsting for success, he was willing to crush anyone who got in his way. Morrie was the man on the make, the American aspirant to riches and power.

Morrie lacked the Karamazov drive to question everything and so become original. Instead he was trapped by the dull character of his goals: money and power. Bellow wrote that his aim in his work was to join low seriousness with high seriousness. The recipe is a traditional one for the novel, and, as in *Don Quixote*, it usually leads to comedy. Morrie had the low seriousness, the thirst for success, but not the high. Not until *Herzog* would Bellow find the winning comic combination of low and high seriousness, in the shape of his autobiographical hero Moses Herzog. But *Augie* was a move in the right direction.

WHEN *The Adventures of Augie March* hit the bookstores in 1953, Bellow was still a struggling young writer. His first two novels had been praised by eminences like Edmund

Wilson and Alfred Kazin, but had sold little. *Dangling Man* and *The Victim* were constricted exercises in modernist angst, adroit and deliberately airless; their heroes were visibly indebted to Dostoevsky's Underground Man and Kafka's Joseph K. Bellow seemed to be in the running to become a grim spokesman for high culture in its tense existentialist mode, a favorite of the *Partisan Review* crowd. Suddenly, his view changed, and with it the future of American fiction. *Augie* was an explosive, shaggy picaresque that offered a comic escape hatch for American writers, an alternative to the recently canonized Faulkner with his tragic, grandly obsessive view of America (Malcolm Cowley's *The Portable Faulkner* had appeared in 1946, seven years before *Augie*).

Bellow decided to jettison the ardent, pure style of existential heroics along with the strict sobrieties of naturalism. He had made a passionate break with the high modernist agenda. *Augie* seemed to its first readers a book that delivered a startling, unkempt newness: the writer was doing things in a new way because this was what reality demanded.

The genesis of *Augie March* occurred in the fall of 1949, when Bellow was living in Paris, his marriage to Anita slowly falling apart. He was working tepidly on a novel about two talkative invalids who conduct a dialogue from their hospital beds (he had tentatively titled the book "The Crab and the Butterfly"). The novel wasn't going well; what Bellow had written was full of long-winded philosophy, and he was depressed over his lack of progress. But another idea for a book kept bothering him, prodding him to attention: something about his early life in Chicago. He called it, for a while, a "speculative biography" rather than a novel; its early chapters resembled a memoir, with all the names changed. Bellow's school friends and their parents appeared, in thinly disguised form; his own family was there too, most of all the hard-driving Morrie. Soon Bellow was sitting in the cafés of Paris and writing furiously, a chapter a week in rough draft. He was having a "wild time," he reported, "stirred to the depths" by his memories.

"IN AMERICAN LITERATURE there were all these strange and homeless solitaries, motherless and fatherless creatures like Natty and Huck and Ishmael. Didn't they know where life came from and returned to?" The question was asked by Irving Howe in "Strangers," a 1977 essay about the Jewish immigrants who, like Howe himself, had grown up talking Yiddish at home but reading and writing American English, who couldn't stop devouring the great American books but all the time wondered why their own lives were so crowded with family—its happiness, its aches and moanings, its staggering disputes—while the lives they were reading about were so stranded and lonely. All the proud Emersonian declarations of individualism, whether pioneer or New England genteel, seemed, by pledging the sublime benefits of isolation, to be a doubtful bill of goods to these hopeful Jewish authors and intellectuals: a denial of *mishpocha* and neighborhood, of the speech-fed chaos that they breathed in and out all day long. How could the Jews, the people of home and family, fit into American fiction, with its outward-bound loners?

Bellow's answer, long before Howe wrote his essay, was *Augie March*. The book was a revelation to writers and readers of American fiction: it was looser, more energetic, more packed with nervous excitement than anything they had seen before. *Augie* was a constantly surprising all-night party in book form, a riposte to the staid *New Yorker* fiction of its day (in a 1951 essay on Dreiser, Bellow had attacked "the 'good' writing of *The New Yorker*": "finally what emerges is a terrible hunger for conformism and uniformity," he wrote). Bellow distanced himself too from the ongoing, artless furies of the Beats: his was a fashioned vividness.

In his long writing career, Bellow discovered that the solitary traveler and the family man could mingle in odd, unprecedented ways; so did Howe, who in "Strangers" jokingly unmasks Melville's Ishmael as a mama's boy. He's really the Isaac of Genesis, Howe claims, doted on endlessly by his mother, Sarah, but he remakes himself into a wild man headed for the far seas: an Ishmael stirred by the jumbled, dangerous world that will lure him away from home forever. Ishmael-Isaac lights out for the territories, but within him all the while is his covenant with the things he first knew, the childhood memories that tell all. So in Bellow, too, the exotic explorer and intellectual highflyer might feel the tug of home. Nostalgia binds us all back to our earliest years.

The Adventures of Augie March is a shaggy-dog story, a cock-and-bull tale, and it wears its shapelessness on its sleeve. In *Augie*, Bellow gives us his most buoyant hero, who combines aspects of Melville's Ishmael, Dickens's David Copperfield, Fielding's Joseph Andrews, and Twain's Huck Finn. When Augie has a dream in which he owns three grand pianos, this flummoxes him, "as I can't play any more than a bull can sew cushions," he says, and we hear Twain's homespun, extravagant Huck.

Augie resembles no other Bellow hero. In his next two big novels, Bellow would invent Henderson, boisterous, large hearted, and utterly out of control, and then manic, sorrowful Herzog, trammeled by two ex-wives and weighed down by the history of ideas. Augie is fresher and more free than these later protagonists: the quintessential young man, a bold yet yielding naïf out to make his way in the world.

Some reviewers found Augie, who bounces back from every mishap, too resilient. Norman Podhoretz in *Commentary* remarked that "Augie reminds us of those animals in the cartoons who get burned to cinders, flattened out like pancakes, exploded, and generally made a mess of, yet who turn up intact after every catastrophe, as if nothing has happened."

Podhoretz missed the unique qualities of *Augie March*. Bellow had brought to a fine pitch what Howe called the "American Jewish style," a style fulfilled, Howe said, in Bellow's work. Howe singled out as key aspects of this style the "forced yoking of opposites: gutter vividness and university refinement"; a "strong infusion of Yiddish" with its "ironic twistings" of phrase; the "deliberate loosening of syntax"; and a technique of playing with common talk so that it "vibrates with cultural ambition, seeking to zoom into the regions of higher thought." In later books like *Herzog, Mr. Sammler's Planet* and *Humboldt's Gift*, Bellow was able to transmit the verbal somersaults of the lecturer gripped by ideas, ravished by his passion for truth and light. And this intellectual questing was combined, as in the great Russian novelists, with a sense of the savage importance of feeling. Augie is relatively isolated from such sufferings and ecstasies, defended by his innocence from the lacerations that ideas can inflict on the soul. But his distinctive patois still marries low and high, with an odd and offhanded range of high cultural references. The piquant Augie sounds grand but not grandiose; his large way of talking is homemade, but never clumsy or pretentious. Bellow's sublime turns are sometimes strangely mated to his reluctant though plucky hero, but they feel right. Bellow ennobles the American language as he skewers it on the spike of immigrant speech. There had been immigrant novels before, from James T. Farrell's brash, jazzy *Studs Lonigan* to Henry Roth's dreamy and impacted *Call It Sleep*, but nothing like this.

Augie is Bellow without the wariness—a little too close, in Bellow's later judgment, to one of Sherwood Anderson's "gee whiz" young men. As Podhoretz noticed, Augie lands on his feet time after time without being especially clever; unlike Bellow himself, he is not canny, he does not keep his eye on the ball. For most of his life, it was hard for Bellow to grasp the link between his own gusto, his greedy taste for experience, and his rapid-fire intelligence, the way he sized up people, places, and ideas for his own purposes. So he created heroes who were either too innocent, like Augie, or too knowing, like Sammler in *Mr. Sammler's Planet.* To be a hard-driving intellectual and an innocent at once was a recipe for trouble: Herzog, Humboldt. Not until his last hero, Ravelstein, did Bellow portray childlike enjoyment and intellectual shrewdness happily married in the same human being. Ravelstein is really just a big kid, one who wants to rule the world.

The question of shrewdness and innocence goes back to how important Morrie was for Bellow. Morrie wanted control, he believed in hard reality, but he lacked the innocence that imagination needs: this, he believed, could only get you in trouble. Morrie's knowingness had nothing intellectual about it, and nothing childlike either. Bellow had to confront his big brother, the most imposing reality instructor in his life, in order to create his later work. He had to overcome the hard realist Morrie, imagination's enemy, so that he could release his later heroes of imagination.

Augie March begins in a house in "Chicago, that somber city," as Bellow names it in his opening sentence (Dreiser in *Sister Carrie* had described Chicago wrapped in a "somber garb of gray"). Grandma Lausch (not a blood relation), who boards with the Marches, rules the roost, teaching Augie "to command, to govern, to manage, scheme, devise and intrigue" as she extracts discounts for the Marches from grocers and peddlers. In the opening pages of *Augie*, Bellow describes Grandma Lausch playing klabyasch, a card game, with a neighbor, Mr. Kreindl, a Hungarian who "was an old-time Austro-Hungarian conscript." "Grandma Lausch played like Timur," reports Augie in a typically far-flung comparison,

> whether chess or klabyasch, with palatal catty harshness and sharp gold in her eyes. Klabyasch she played with Mr. Kreindl, a neighbor of ours who had taught her the game. A powerful stub-handed man with a large belly, he swatted the table with those hard hands of his, flinging down his cards and shouting, "*Shtoch! Yasch! Menél! Klabyasch!*"

(In rough translation from Yiddish and Polish: "Ouch, that hurts! The trump! You bum! Klabyasch!") The scene will be instantly recognizable to anyone who grew up in an immigrant household where games like pinochle, chess and klabyasch (also known as clabber) provided a stage for high-handed theater.

Augie's father has deserted the family and his mother is nearly invisible, so Grandma Lausch is the de facto head of the March family. She sends Augie running to the public library for the novels she devours, and reprimands him when he brings her back, by mistake, a Tolstoy religious tract ("How many times do I have to tell you if it doesn't say *roman* I don't want it?") She reigns through intimidation, and is hard-hearted too: she consigns the Marches' mentally disabled little brother, Georgie, to a home for the feeble-minded—and then is herself forced to move to an old age home, where she loses her memory along with her powers of manipulation. Augie is dismayed by Grandma Lausch's signs of triumph after she has dispatched Georgie: "the old lady made of it something it didn't necessarily have to be, a test of strength, tactless, a piece of sultanism," the product of an "angry giddiness from self-imposed, prideful struggle." Bellow might have been thinking of Morrie when he wrote these lines. Grandma Lausch's greedy desire to triumph over others is like Morrie's, and Augie rejects it. Instead he sides with the weak of the world, people like his poor brother Georgie. Augie himself is a drifter, passive and lucky. His interest in the powerful is tender and curious, but he can't quite see their point. His innocence protects him from the rapacious schemers.

Early in his career Augie falls in with his cousins, the Coblins, and encounters Anna Coblin's brother, the Cyclops-like Five Properties, so named for the landlord's boast he prides himself on, part of his routine pitch to girls. (Was Bellow thinking of Dostoevsky's Ptitsyn in *The Idiot*, who could never rank more than four houses?)

> That would be Five Properties shambling through the cottage, Anna's immense brother, long armed and humped, his head grown off the thick band of muscle as original as a bole on his back, hair tender and greenish brown, eyes completely green, clear, estimating, primitive, and sardonic, an Eskimo smile of primitive simplicity opening on Eskimo teeth

buried in high gums, kidding, gleeful, and unfrank;
a big-footed contender for wealth.

This passage reveals much about Bellow's new style in *Augie March*, so radically different from the taut, measured rhythms of his first two novels. Bellow is here as rough and loping as Five Properties himself, and rhapsodic too. You can imagine Whitman delivering that "clear, estimating, primitive, and sardonic." Bellow piles up adjectives as high as Five Properties' bulky, clever head. He twines together Five Properties' cunning nature with his fresh high spirits: both childlike and cynical, he is "kidding, gleeful, and unfrank." Always in Bellow, someone's body tells you all about his soul: physiognomy is destiny. So it is with Five Properties and his Eskimo mouth, which carries both smiling heartiness and strenuous, testing ambition. "What he had to say was usually on the Spartan or proconsular model, quick and hard," Augie says of Five Properties; for a girl, he "had in mind a bouncing, black-haired, large-lipped, party-going peach." Bellow's portrait of Five Properties, in a few quick strokes, is complete: striving, sly, blunt, out for pleasure and power.

Five Properties is Morrie without his grossness and violence: a gentle brute. There's a telling difference between Bellow's attitude toward such a figure and that of his inheritor Philip Roth, who takes the will to personal power altogether more earnestly, more ascetically. For Bellow, those who want power necessarily court the outlandish. Five Properties is cartoonlike, but also winningly personable; there is nothing sterile or self-enclosed about him. By contrast, Roth's people are brilliantly stunted. They nurture their desires like prize possessions, jealously guarding them.

In a telling 1984 letter to Roth, Bellow summed up the difference between them: "You seem to have accepted the Freudian explanation: a writer is motivated by his desire for fame, money and sexual opportunities. Whereas I have never taken this trinity of motives seriously." There is a high romantic conviction in Bellow that never appears in Roth: Bellow thinks that the self aims for expression, on as wild and full a canvas as possible, rather than control. The characters Roth creates are tightly possessive as they pursue power over women, over themselves. Bellow's people, by contrast, when they desire riches, fame or sex, seem like kids. They are set loose rather than cramped by what they want. It took time for Bellow to reach this freedom, and the first step toward it was to surpass the clenched, hungry egoism of Morrie, who was really a Roth character rather than a Bellow one.

———

AUGIE HOLDS DOWN a series of odd jobs, from dog walking to shoplifting textbooks. He also dallies with a number of women, including a Greek union organizer named Sophie and the wealthy, temperamental Thea Fenchel. Bellow had a deep crush on a girl really named Fenchel in high school; in *Augie*, he turned the tables, making her fall in love with him instead. (Decades later, at a Tuley High School reunion, Fenchel's husband rose from his wheelchair to slap Bellow for flirting with his wife.)

Midway through the novel, Augie helps a friend, Mimi, get an abortion. It's hard to think of another account of an abortion by a male writer that displays such sympathy and such realism, and such dark comedy. When Augie takes Mimi to a hospital, they are treated with contempt. In another part of the book, Augie rides the rails: a dusky, gritty Depression-era scene. Eventually he departs for Mexico with Thea, who is determined to train an eagle to hunt giant iguanas. When Augie heads for Mexico, the novel turns riskier and more rhapsodic, and at times feels rather aimless.

And so Bellow's Augie keeps rolling. After his return from Mexico, he joins the Merchant Marine, as Bellow did near the end of World War II. He gets engaged to Stella, a girl he met south of the border, and through her he encounters Mintouchian, a high-powered Armenian lawyer. As it nears its end, *Augie March* revives tremendously with Mintouchian, a reality instructor to rival the Stein of Conrad's *Lord Jim*. He is, Bellow writes, "a monument of a person, with his head very abrupt at the back, as Armenian heads tend sometimes to be, but lionlike in front, with red cheekbones." Dressed usually "in evening clothes of Rembrandt blackness," Mintouchian will give Augie a dose of dark yet vitalizing wisdom.

The sage Armenian *macher* Mintouchian tells Augie that "the thing that kills you is the thing that you stand for": "What is the weapon? The nails and hammer of your character. What is the cross? Your own bones on which you gradually weaken. . . . The fish wills water, and the bird wills air, and you and me our dominant idea." "You must take your chance on what you are," he commands Augie, and—sounding like Emerson—"only system taps the will of the universe." As a juiced-up, sharp-eyed lawyer, Mintouchian is supremely aware of the human bent for deception (much of his talk concerns philandering). Yet he convincingly recommends to Augie a magnificent self-trust. For a few pages, he solves the puzzle of Bellow's protean, seemingly endless book, making it come to rest in a settled place, high romantic and sure of itself.

Even better is yet to come. A few pages later in *Augie March*, Bellow scuttles Mintouchian's wisdom, replacing the grand Armenian with an uncanny zany out of Dostoevsky: a lunatic ship's carpenter and autodidact scientist named Basteshaw. In an episode that seems sprouted from a *New Yorker* cartoon (and my own favorite stretch of the novel), Augie and Basteshaw find themselves adrift on the wide ocean after their Merchant Marine vessel is shipwrecked, and for days on end Basteshaw bombards Augie with his ardent theories. Basteshaw is something of a low-rent Nietzschean, who fantasized in college about being a Renaissance cardinal—"A wicked one, smoking with life, neighing and plunging"—but who then laid aside such titillation in order to pursue a scholarly project: to become the world's greatest expert on boredom. Augie is "stupefied" by Basteshaw's coolly assured lecturer's manner: "I watched him climb around like an alpinist of the mountains of his own brain, sturdy, and with his calm goggles and his blue glances of certitude." Finally, Basteshaw quietly reveals his secret: while monkeying around in his lab with protoplasm, he created life. (Here Bellow is spoofing the psychoanalyst Wilhelm Reich, one of his early enthusiasms: Reich claimed he had discovered the elementary units of life, which he called "bions.")

Like the addled Basteshaw—whose ideas are both insane and, in the end, rather infectious—Bellow created life when he wrote *Augie*. Lionel Trilling's judgment of *Augie March*, expressed in a letter to Bellow's editor, was glowing. "It's Saul's gift to see life everywhere," Trilling wrote to Pat Covici. "He really believes in the living will. There isn't an inert person in the book, just as there isn't an inert sentence." Trilling recommended the novel with enthusiasm in an essay that later became the introduction to the Modern Library edition of *Augie*. Bellow was grateful for such praise, but he knew that *Augie* wasn't really Trilling's kind of book. Neither judicious nor weighted with maturity, *Augie March* careens, often gloriously hits, but sometimes misses.

In a letter to Bernard Malamud Bellow admitted *Augie March*'s flaws: "I made many mistakes. . . . Yes, Augie is too passive, perhaps. Yes, the episodes do not have enough variety." But Bellow was proud of what he had done, the form he had chosen. "A novel, like a letter, should be loose, cover much ground, run swiftly," he wrote to Malamud. "[In *Augie*] I backed away from Flaubert, in the direction of Balzac, Walter Scott and Dickens." Bellow's looseness of form made possible an appreciation of the human presences that inhabit a novel; in contrast, tightly controlled Flaubertian modernism privileged the author who loomed high over his characters. (In a 1960 essay, "The Sealed Treasure," Bellow criticized the Flaubertian style's "disappointment with its human material.")

Augie March gives us the novel as an unruly creature, shining and messy; it lets in more of life, in unfiltered form, than readers had been used to. Neither Hemingway with his narrow artistic code (which, Bellow once complained, leaves so much of life out) nor Faulkner with his drenched operatic intensity, which seems to artificially heighten everything it touches, could have accomplished this. Bellow perfected a new, more open style: distinctively Jewish in the ways that Howe noticed but at the same time harking back to Melville, Twain, and Emerson.

Augie March eventually sold thirty thousand copies: not quite a best seller, but good; and it won the National Book Award. The novel made Bellow famous. Flush with his new success, he sent a copy of *Augie* to his father. Abraham Bellow wrote to his son proudly from Chicago, "The book made a hit all over America. I hope the next will be still better," and continued: "Still from time to time send me few lines a letter. . . . Still I am the head of all of you. Pa Bellow."

Bellow found his father's praise less than satisfying. Writing to his high school friend Sam Freifeld in the fall of 1953, after the success of *Augie*, Bellow commented, "It's just like my father to begin to be generous long after the rest of the world has begun. He's impressed by my new fame and even more by the sales of the book and now he feels uneasy and wants, too late, to go on record as a good parent. I try to make him feel that there is plenty of time."

Bellow avoided depicting his father's furious temperament in his published work. But he continued his struggle with Morrie long after *Augie March*. In a book-length manuscript from the fifties, "Memoirs of a Bootlegger's Son," Bellow tried to tell his family's story through a narrator who combines aspects of Morrie and Saul, but the project was a failure, and Bellow published only a brief section from it. Two decades later, *Humboldt's Gift* was another story: here Bellow produced a moving, elegiac study of the aging Morrie. In *Humboldt* the Morrie character, Charlie Citrine's elder brother Ulick, becomes a sufferer rather than the manipulator he was in *Augie*. Bellow knew that Morrie had a self-punishing streak as well as a wish to punish others. He wrote to Freifeld in 1953, "A few years ago when my brother had cancer he cried out, 'I pissed my life away!' And now look at him. That's all forgotten. But I didn't forget the great pain of hearing a man condemn himself. . . . Of course, so long as our misery is secret our honor is whole." Morrie had a nervous turmoil inside him, just like Bellow, who was also haunted by the specter of failure. Not until *Herzog*, published when he was nearly fifty, did Bellow become financially secure. Both brothers worried that their immense confidence might be covering a pit of self-doubt.

In *Humboldt's Gift* Bellow produces his most affecting portrait of Morrie. In his sixties Ulick has moved south, as Morrie did—to Texas rather than Morrie's Georgia. He has become a real estate man, "one of the biggest builders of southeast Texas." Facing major heart surgery, he puts "on a shirt of flame-blue Italian silk, a beautiful garment," and devours fish and persimmons with his brother Charlie, who has come down to see him before the operation. "We sat with him under a tree sucking at the breast-sized, flame-colored fruit. The juice spurted over his sport shirt, and seeing that it now had to go to the cleaner anyway he wiped his fingers on it as well. His eyes had shrunk, and moved back and forth rapidly in his head." Ulick, in an "ecstasy of craftiness," is still plotting real estate deals. "It seemed to me there were few faces like his," Charlie says, "with the ferocious profile that brought to mind the Latin word *rapax* or one of Rouault's crazed death-dealing arbitrary kings." Charlie remembers Ulick the child: "I still saw in him the obese, choked-looking boy, the lustful conniving kid whose eyes continually pleaded not guilty. I knew him inside-out. . . . I knew the mole on the back of his wrist, his nose broken and reset, his fierce false look of innocence, his snorts, and his smells." "If I die on the table," Ulick tells Charlie, he wants Charlie to marry his wife, Hortense. (Ulick will survive the operation.) "Arrogant, haggard, he was filled with incommunicable thoughts." In *Humboldt's Gift* Ulick—Morrie—has become an isolated, proud king, self-shuttered, shadowed by death. His greedy eating habits have something desperate about them.

Bellow concludes Charlie's meeting with Ulick with a few unsteady sentences: "Late noon stood like a wall of gold. And a mass of love was between us, and neither Ulick nor I knew what to do with it. 'Well, all right, good-by.' He turned his back on me. I got into the rented car and took off."

The sentiment is overripe, as if to make up for Ulick's silence. Charlie talks plangently about their "mass of love" because he knows that Ulick won't. The novelist, faced with his hard, restless brother, cannot avoid the sentimental openness that Morrie scorned. Morrie turned his back on his brother. Was Bellow trying to reach him or exorcise him by evoking their shared childhood past in his work? Something of both, no doubt. As long as he lived, Bellow was still, like Augie, the innocent kid faced with a wised-up older brother, the original reality instructor.

CHAPTER 2

Ralph Ellison

"YOU KNOW I carry a knife," Ralph Ellison sometimes liked to say when he sensed a fight might be brewing at a party. Ellison never pulled his knife, but he wanted people to think there was something dangerous lurking beneath his composed, steely-yet-mild exterior. The parties, in New York or Princeton or at Bard College, were mostly populated by intellectuals like Ellison, almost all of them, unlike Ellison, white. It was a long way from Oklahoma City, Ellison's hometown, where he had heard the satisfying, bold voice of Jimmy Rushing wafting down the streets, where he snuck into juke joints, and where he became a professional-grade trumpet player as a teenager.

For Bellow, Ellison was the anti-Morrie: a man of style, elegant not brutal, unashamedly taking the side of culture. He and Bellow became close friends in the early fifties in New York, when Ellison was writing his masterpiece *Invisible Man* and Bellow was writing *Augie March*. Bellow thought that Ellison resembled a Hemingway type, showing grace under pressure—the natural aristocrat, the man under control. Nowhere in Bellow's fiction does such a man appear. Bellow was simply unable to depict Ellison. He was too quiet, too subtle, for a Bellow novel. But Ellison's stylish composure exerted a pull on Bellow nevertheless. Being with Ellison helped Bellow define himself as Ellison's opposite: a man of shreds and patches, brimming with love and rage, thirsty for actual human presence. Ellison was peculiarly unable to describe love in his work, and his anger was crafty, hidden like his knife. Bellow's passion was all on the surface, bursting out. Ellison's invisible man was a subterranean, born to silence, exile, and cunning. Henderson and Herzog would have access to none of these weapons. Instead they were wide open, their lives unruly, confused.

There was a temperamental kinship between Bellow and Ellison. Bellow, like Ellison, preferred to keep his guard up; he often had the wary self-protective manner that Roth described in *The Ghost Writer.* Once, at a Rice University dinner in Houston, Bellow turned to the writer Max Apple and asked in Yiddish, *"Vos voln zey fun mir?"*—"What do they want from me?" Bellow's defensive streak ran deep. Ellison showed him a way of defending oneself that would not be cagey and fraught but solid, dignified. Yet the two men were separated by their career paths. Within a few years after the success of *Invisible Man*, Ellison, his creative work a shambles, was falling apart within. He would never publish another novel, whereas Bellow's career kept ascending.

Like Bellow, Ellison came from working people. He was born in Oklahoma City in 1913 (he would later shave a year off his age and say 1914). When Ellison was three, his father, who delivered ice and coal, lost his grip on a huge block of ice, a shard pierced his abdomen, and he eventually died from the wound. The boy Ellison was with his father when the accident happened, and he remembered forever the visits to his dying father in the hospital. Ellison's father had little money, but he loved books, and he had literary ambitions for his son, so he had named him Ralph Waldo Ellison. For the rest of his life, Ellison was nervously and proudly conscious of the distinction his father intended for him. Bellow, whose mother died when he was a teenager, yearns in his fiction after women with maternal talents who can soothe the anxious, fast-thinking male. Ellison, who lost his father as a child, invented in his work a series of male authority figures, all of them lacking in one way or another. As for women, they were a minor presence: sex is nearly absent in *Invisible Man*, as if under a taboo.

At twenty Ellison left Oklahoma for Tuskegee Institute, where he studied music composition. He decided that, like his idol Wagner, he would have his first symphony performed before he reached age twenty-six. That ambition didn't quite pan out: Ellison had talent as a composer, but not enough. In 1936, after three years at Tuskegee, Ellison left without a degree and drifted north until he hit Harlem. He left music for painting, photography, and then, at last, writing. He worked for the Federal Writers' Project, wrote for the Communist-aligned *New Masses*, and got to know

Richard Wright, who first urged him to try his hand at writing fiction. In the early forties, disillusioned with the Party, he became an ally of the intellectuals who had turned their backs on Stalinism. Like Bellow, he was a youthful leftist who changed his stripes and embraced anti-Communist liberalism.

"It all began during the summer of 1945, in a barn in Waitsfield, Vermont," Ellison recalled. He was on sick leave from the Merchant Marine. Walking through the Vermont village he saw a poster for a "Tom show," a blackface rendition of *Uncle Tom's Cabin*. Ellison imagined he heard a "taunting, disembodied voice" reminding him of the image-ridden history of black life in America. In Vermont Ellison was possessed by the idea that something central about African American life might be captured through a voice from underground, a voice inspired by one of the many "superfluous men" who populated the Russian novels that Ellison adored. Dostoevsky's *Notes from Underground* seemed to Ellison the right model for what he started on that summer in Vermont: a monologue by a hidden, haunted young black man, who later became the hero of *Invisible Man*. To be black in America, Ellison knew, was to be ignored, slighted, and unseen, even though color was the first, maybe the only, thing most people noticed about you.

Ellison had realized an astonishing fact about our country: that African Americans are invisible not just to whites, but at times even to one another. Because to be African American is to be reduced to the appearance of blackness, the black man or woman becomes a sign rather than a living reality—born to be looked through, an ambulating ghost. Yet America, Ellison saw with a shock, couldn't be explained any other way than through blackness, so potent was the role the slaves and their descendants had played in the nation's culture.

Ellison started writing his novel in Vermont, and he continued when he returned to New York later in 1945. The world war was over, and Ellison's questions about the future of our racially divided country began to sink in. His book was about a young, unnamed black man "bent upon finding his way in areas of society whose manners, motives and rituals were baffling," Ellison wrote years later. The novel's hero was neither a firebrand seeking self-realization Emerson style, nor one of Hemingway's stoics standing a manly test, but an unformed youth who seemed notably—pardon the joke—colorless.

"No, I am not a spook like those who haunted Edgar Allan Poe," Ellison's protagonist tells the reader on his first page, but rather someone you meet, though without noticing him, all the time. The world the invisible man travels through is not nightmarish or surreal, but oddly normal. The low-key nature of *Invisible Man* proves all-important: Ellison refuses melodrama in order to show us the plain and palpable strangeness of a society that sees everywhere a polar contrast between black and white. When the color line defines everything, yet runs through nothing deeper than mere physical appearance, we enter a story weird as any science fiction. But because much of American history tells this story, we have long since stopped thinking about the disturbingly unreal idea of race that lies behind it.

Readers of *Invisible Man* have often felt that they can slip into the skin of Ellison's protagonist with no effort at all. I remember talking about the book some years ago to a high school class in Harlem that had just read *Hamlet* and now was on to *Invisible Man*. "I like Hamlet because he has chutzpah," one girl in the class sweetly remarked, but there is no one in literature less chutzpahdik than Ellison's unnamed hero. Even when he stirs things up late in the book by making an incendiary speech in the streets of Harlem, he seems to be doing nothing at all. He is a mere bystander at the conflagration. The oddly absent quality of Ellison's hero spoke to me when I first encountered *Invisible Man* as a teenager, and it continues to send its uncanny message whenever I read it again in middle age. The central figures of Bellow's first two novels, Joseph in *Dangling Man* and Asa Leventhal in *The Victim*, are similarly slight in stature, background men who find themselves unexpectedly in the foreground. Bellow, like Ellison, began his career by depicting superfluous people.

Ellison could be prickly, he was often a hard drinker, and he found it easy, even diverting, to infuriate people. All these traits—except the drinking—Ellison shared with Bellow. When Ellison was writing *Invisible Man*, his intellectual circle was the mostly Jewish *Partisan Review* crowd, and Bellow was his main compatriot among that group of writers and critics. Ellison and his wife, Fanny, often visited Bellow and Anita in their apartment in Forest Hills, and the two novelists liked to go fishing with Bellow's son Greg tagging along. Ellison built a hi-fi system for Bellow's birthday (a committed tinkerer, Ellison loved electronics, a fact reflected in the invisible man's intricately rigged basement). At this time, in the very early fifties, the Bellows were flat broke, and Saul and Anita were barely talking to each other. Their sojourn in Mexico, marked by brief affairs on both sides, had strained their marriage. Bellow's philandering was constant, and it deeply distressed Anita. The once young novelist, now pushing forty, felt pent up by bourgeois existence and confined by lack of money. Bellow had started Reichian therapy, egged on by his friend Isaac Rosenfeld. Twice a week he lay naked on the therapist's couch and roared like a lion, "being my animal self," he said.

While Ellison was wrapping up *Invisible Man* (an effort that so exhausted him that, he said later, he had to lie in bed for weeks afterward), Bellow was putting the finishing touches on *Augie March*. *Invisible Man* was published in 1952, hit the best seller lists, and won the National Book Award. *Augie March*, which came out the following year, also won the National Book Award, though Bellow had to wait eleven more years for his first best seller, *Herzog*.

While Bellow and Ellison waited for their fame, they had *Partisan Review* to argue over and, sometimes, to write for. Bellow's fledgling short stories had appeared there in the early forties, and in 1952 the magazine published Ellison's "Invisible Man: Prologue to a Novel," the first taste of his forthcoming masterpiece. *Partisan Review* was the home of the anti-Communist left, and also the home base for worshippers of the European avant-garde who were trying to transplant such cutting-edge art to America. The world capital of visual art was moving from Paris to New York, and *Partisan Review*'s trailblazing critics, Clement Greenberg and Harold Rosenberg, worked hard to make that westward migration occur. The titanic Rosenberg, a whirlwind of bold speech and thinking, walked with a limp from a childhood illness and was an endless source of verbal and intellectual fireworks; he became a lifelong friend to Bellow.

Bellow later cracked that the editors of *Partisan Review* had the mentality of Sixth Avenue cigar importers, but, he added, at least what they were importing, European culture, was worth something. Yet Bellow and Ellison stood apart from the other members of the *Partisan Review* group because they thought that America had plenty of cultural resources of its own. What joined Bellow and Ellison together was their sense that Americans, including Jewish and black Americans, had something to say for themselves quite apart from European models. True, Ellison revered Malraux and Bellow was soaked in Tolstoy (Bellow's son Adam told me that his father reread *War and Peace* every year). They had absorbed the lessons of Dostoevsky, Conrad, Joyce, and Dickens. But at a "little lower layer," as Captain Ahab put it, they knew themselves to be sons of Melville and, especially, Mark Twain, the first writer to make American colloquial speech the very substance of his novels. Twain made no apologies for America's lack of the highfalutin manners and high-art traditions of Europe.

America had something of its own, Twain argued: an illiterate slave or a mixed-up teenage boy from the Missouri frontier might be as distinguished as any duchess. Twain's lesson would be unmistakable to both Bellow and Ellison as they thought about how their American upbringing, whether in its Jewish or its black variation, was going to enter into the books they would write.

Ellison and the Jewish writers who surrounded him cross-fertilized one another, most of all in the questions they asked themselves. Does it make sense to talk about "authentic" blackness or Jewishness? Is authenticity an outworn concept, and if so, what might replace it? Are folk tale and history the keys to a people's identity? What happens when folk habits fade and histories are forgotten? These were matters that both Jews and African Americans wrestled with. Like the Jewish writers, Ellison wanted to go beyond just documenting the customs of his tribe. Ethnic life was something more subtle and encompassing, a whole way of being, even when it blended with the larger culture's ways.

Invisible Man catapulted Ellison into celebrity. Instantly he was the most famous black author in America. Bellow in his *Commentary* review called *Invisible Man* "a superb book, a book of the very first order." The review cemented the connection between Ellison and Bellow. In April 1955, Ellison wrote in a letter to his friend Albert Murray that he'd been "having once a week sessions with Bellow, listening to him read from his work-in-progress and reading to him from mine. For about thirty minutes we cuss out all the sonsabitches who say the novel's dead, then we read and discuss." A few months later, in July, Ellison took part in a panel discussion called "What's Wrong with the American Novel?" He criticized Hemingway for his narrow fixation on technique and he came down hard on Wright for his addiction to sociology. But he praised Bellow, the author of *Augie March*, as the rightful successor to Faulkner. When *Augie March* had appeared two years earlier, Ellison remarked to Wright that it was "the first real novel by an American Jew."

One could say something similar about *Invisible Man*: that with all due respect to Wright's *Native Son*, it was the first real novel by an African American. *Invisible Man* let loose the imagination, unlike *Native Son*, which kept to a flat naturalist style sprinkled with melodrama and social protest. Ellison the novelist, like Zora Neale Hurston in her then little noticed *Their Eyes Were Watching God*, did what the sociologist W. E. B. Du Bois could not do in *The Souls of Black Folk*: draw on the passing currents of African American talk and manners to make a permanent work of art. Ellison accomplished for black America what Faulkner had done for the white South—he fashioned its epic.

To understand Bellow, we need to take a deeper look at *Invisible Man*, since Bellow thought about Ellison's work with an intensity he gave to no other of his fellow authors, at a time when he was still figuring out his own path. Ellison's novel charts the journey of a naïve black youth from a Tuskegee-like university in the South up to Harlem, where he becomes a rabble-rouser for the Communist Party, called the Brotherhood in the novel. The unnamed protagonist becomes disillusioned with the Brotherhood, and rejects his budding career as a left-wing orator. Instead of Frederick Douglass, he turns into a Kafkaesque burrower. He escapes from a race riot in Harlem by popping into a sewer, and ends the book by retreating into a subterranean lair lit by 1369 lightbulbs. There he watches and waits: for what, he does not quite know.

Invisible Man's momentous last line is "Who knows but that, on the lower frequencies, I speak for you?" The "you" in that sentence is anyone, black or white, who can smell the air and discern that the time might soon be ripe to slide down the hatch, to hide out and stay wary. Ellison's novel broadcast the dark signals running beneath the tame surface of the fifties. Ellison challenged us to tune in, not to a high Emersonian pitch, but to a low-down portent of future strife, not to aspire, but to lay low like Jack the Bear. The invisible man, that nondescript *Kleinmensch*, is actually a sophisticated human antenna getting a radio station the rest of us can't yet hear. Even belowground and unseen, he knows which way the wind blows, and possesses the key for times to come. There is an edge of prophecy in the final pages of Ellison's great novel, an omen of future pestilence: *Invisible Man*'s closing race riot presages the wildfires of rebellion that would sweep across the country little more than a decade after the book was published.

Most of Ellison's spectacular set pieces occur early on in *Invisible Man*. Taken together, they feel like the heart of the book. First comes the Battle Royal, a stag party in which young black men are teased by a naked white blonde, then forced to fight each other in front of a rich white audience. Then there's the Trueblood episode, in which the hero, now at college, takes a wealthy white donor to the shack of an incestuous sharecropper. Trueblood mesmerizes and sickens the white man with his monologue about having sex with his own daughter. Ellison uses Trueblood's speech as a send-up of the traumatic revelations in Greek tragedy, but also an homage to the sly, rough and tumble powers of black speech, which, when Trueblood speaks it, can recognize and make light of horrors in the same breath. Bellow would devise voices just as marvelous, from Mintouchian in *Augie* to *Humboldt*'s Cantabile, but none of them have what one hears in Ellison's Trueblood: the sheer terrifying freedom drawn from a personal doom.

Trueblood is comic and repellent at once, a folk monster out of the country blues, the music whose profound tones ripple through his speech. Even more memorable is Bledsoe, the masterful head of the black college. Proud, cynical, insidious, Bledsoe appears to kowtow to white power but in fact manipulates the white world for his own purposes. Bledsoe punishes the invisible man in underhanded, cruel fashion. He expels him from school after the Trueblood debacle, then sends him north with false letters of recommendation urging the recipient to deny him a job. His biographer Arnold Rampersad writes that Ellison saw Bledsoe as "the epitome of Negro psychological and even spiritual ingenuity in response to white terror." Bledsoe is the closest thing to the devil in Ellison's novel, and like the devil he exerts an uncanny charm. He is a powerful potential father, and the invisible man fails this father's test. Ellison's young hero is not hard enough, not deceptive enough—in short, not bad enough—to be a Bledsoe. So Bledsoe kicks him out, and the invisible man comes close to being nobody at all. Here, as always, Ellison's novel is full of the risk that a black man encounters in a white world. Bellow's *Augie March* is never treacherous like Ellison's book. Like the invisible man, Bellow's wholehearted Augie lacks cunning and real-world pith, but unlike Ellison's hero, he thrives.

In his forty-year-long career of essay writing after *Invisible Man*, Ellison often argued that African Americans do not live in a sealed bubble—a "jug," as he put it. To think so would be downright un-American, and deeply mistaken. He never tired of reiterating that white Americans are who they are in part because of black style and artistry, black ways of talking and being. "You cannot have an American experience without having a black experience," Ellison wrote in one of his essays. The same could surely be said of America and Jewish experience.

"*All* us old-fashioned Negroes are Jews," Ellison once remarked in an interview. He was responding to Leslie Fiedler's jibe that Ellison was, as Fiedler put it at one panel discussion in 1969, "a black Jew." Fiedler probably meant that Ellison was too immersed in the world of the New York intellectuals, not sufficiently tied to his people. But Ellison turned Fiedler's snap into a compliment. As he saw it, blacks and Jews shared a few traits that were admirable and, for an underdog, crucial: a shrewd, self-reliant, practical sense of the world, an ingrained distrust of stiff and pompous ways, and most of all that essential survival strategy, the ability to keep one's cool. Fiedler and his like just didn't get it. The white leftist critic wanted blacks to be righteously angry. If they weren't, then they just weren't black enough—at least that was Ellison's take on Fiedler's impromptu ribbing.

In his essay "The World and the Jug," written in 1963, eleven years after *Invisible Man*, Ellison described some of the characteristics that African Americans had relied on to survive among whites: "Their resistance to provocation, their coolness under pressure, their sense of timing and their tenacious hold on the ideal of their ultimate freedom." The essay was a response to Irving Howe's "Black Boys and Native Sons," an attack on Ellison in which Howe suggested that Wright's blunt anger, not Ellison's suave and resourceful manner, was the proper answer to the brutal conditions of black American life. Swinging with the punches, staying cool, acting free even when one wasn't: none of these traits were valuable in Howe's eyes, Ellison implies, at least when it came to African Americans. Although Howe had memorably praised the comic resilience of Sholem Aleichem's Tevye, he preferred his black characters hate-filled and vindictive. In black life the authentic was the raw, the slice of reality so narrow that, for Ellison, it ceased to be real. Howe, Ellison damagingly wrote, was "carried away by that intellectual abandon, that lack of restraint, which seizes those who regard blackness as an absolute and see in it a release from the complications of the world."

Being Jewish was, for Ellison, similar to being black: not an absolute fact but a complicated one. Jews knew something more, lived something more, than most whites, he thought. In some ways, Jews didn't seem white at all. Ellison remarked in "The World and the Jug," "Speaking personally, both as writer and as Negro American, I would like to see the more positive distinctions between whites and Jewish Americans maintained." The closeness Ellison felt with Jewish Americans, so visible in his friendship with Bellow, was striking, and set him apart from the Black Power generation that succeeded him (in the sixties, black activists frequently and cruelly accused Ellison of being an Uncle Tom).

Ellison felt at home with liberal Jews, then, more than with radical black leftists. He knew Yiddish, too, and not just a little. He must have picked up the language when, as a boy, he worked at Lewisohn's Department Store in Oklahoma City. According to Arnold Rampersad's biography, one of Ellison's New England summer-home neighbors, Harriet Davidson, reported that Ellison "and my husband would sit on the porch and converse very easily in Yiddish. Ralph had no trouble speaking or understanding it." This is another thing that brought Ellison and Bellow together: Yiddish was Bellow's native language, and he spoke it to the end of his life.

In a 1955 letter to Ruth Miller, his future biographer, Bellow discussed Ellison's and his own writing in tandem. The first third of *Invisible Man* is "beautiful," Bellow wrote to Miller, but the novel's later section on the Brotherhood is "ordinary," because it so strenuously looks for meaning. "I think this is a fault of all American books, including my own," Bellow continued. "They pant so after meaning . . . they exhort and plead and refine, and they are, insofar, books of error." Bellow went on to trace this error to two masters of modernist prose, Proust and James: the "original guilty parties," with their "passion for adding meaning to meaning in a work of art, and *making* meaning proliferate from ordinary incidents." Bellow, who late in life derived, he said, considerable *naches* from reading Proust, added, "Let us assume that Proust at least could not help himself. But this is a hanging matter with James, and with the rest of us." Bellow was trying to slay the devil of contrivance, of making meaning, a devil to whom, he thought, Ellison had sold his soul.

Bellow's anti-modernist battle cry in his letter to Miller was that "writing should derive from the Creation, and not attempt to add to it. We should require things to be simpler and simpler, greater and greater." He is being true to one of his favorite aphorisms, which he cited in *Humboldt's Gift*: Tolstoy's exhortation that we must cease the false and unnecessary comedy of history and begin simply to live. Tolstoy himself, of course, worked history into the vast fabric of *War and Peace*, but on every page of that great work, he transmitted his sense that when we think about history, we assume false, too-grand postures. Ideas about the large-scale meaning of nationalism, communism, or any other ism can never hold true to the fact of our passions and our characters, the human essence that shows in how we cook an egg, smash a plate, or talk to a child. Ideas surround us, we swim in them, but they frustrate too. They can never get us far enough into life, and so we desperately wish to break through them and begin simply to live. Tolstoy's Levin, who is in part the sublime Russian novelist's alter ego, embodies this wish for pure life, unfettered by the ideas that throw an interfering shadow between us and our experiences.

As Bellow saw it, Ellison bogged down in his attempt to write the follow-up to *Invisible Man* because he had succumbed to the urge to make things idea-bound, dense and complex rather than simple. He was searching for the meaning that he thought would spring from symbol and allegory; for him, every object was a golden bowl. He began to use Joycean stream of consciousness, and to litter his work with allusions. Such manipulations worked for Joyce, but they became a dangerous precedent, drawing so many novelists after Joyce away from life with its awkward simplicities. For Bellow, the Dreiser of *Jennie Gerhardt*, clumsy as his prose may have been at times, was a better guide than Joyce and Woolf. Dreiser's people *lived*. Because they were themselves, they did not need to be symbols of anything. Joyce wanted to make his characters' thoughts interesting; Dreiser was too primal to need to do this, since for him human personalities were worthy from the start. Already toward the end of *Invisible Man*, Ellison had started down the wrong road: his Brother Jack and Brother Tarp were not people but mouthpieces for ideas.

THE BOND BETWEEN Ellison and Bellow was at its most intense in the late fifties. During these years Ellison was on the slow mend. Since 1955 he had been a fellow of the American Academy in Rome, where he had a serious love affair that turned disastrous. Bellow too was in pain. He had suffered a string of losses: his father's death in 1955, his divorce from his first wife, Anita, the same year, and the death the following year of his best friend, the exuberant writer and critic Isaac Rosenfeld, at the tragically early age of thirty-eight.

There was exhilaration for Bellow too during these difficult years. He had fallen rapturously in love with the glamorous Sondra Tschacbasov, a Bennington grad who was working as a receptionist at the *Partisan Review.* "I could have gone out with Philip Rahv or Saul," she recalled later. "I chose Saul." After their marriage broke up, Bellow portrayed Sondra as a neurotic, high-strung manipulator in *Herzog*, a con artist of the soul, but for the time being he was head over heels.

In 1956 Bellow married Sondra in Reno. After the wedding, in a cabin at the edge of the desert, he read aloud to the assembled guests from the novel that would become *Henderson the Rain King. Henderson*, which came out three years later, is a crazy romp through Africa taken by a rich, roughhousing Connecticut Yankee, the steepest roller-coaster ride among all Bellow's books. While he was writing his wild saga, Bellow said to Ellison in a letter that he didn't "know which parts of the book originate in gaiety and which in desperation."

Bellow had been living in Reno so that he could get a divorce from Anita; Arthur Miller was there for the same reason. Miller, along with his fiancée, Marilyn Monroe, occupied the cottage next to Bellow. He remembered the novelist standing behind a hill and "emptying his lungs roaring at the stillness": a vigorous Reichian shout worthy of Henderson himself. A few years later, Bellow and Sondra sometimes met Miller and Monroe in New York for double dates—Greg Bellow remembers Sondra advising Marilyn about what to wear before the two couples went out together in Little Italy. "I have yet to see anything in Marilyn that isn't genuine," Bellow wrote his editor, Pat Covici. "Surrounded by thousands she conducts herself like a philosopher."

In October 1956 Ellison, AWOL from the American Academy and depressed over his affair in Rome, had lunch with Bellow and Sondra in New York. Bellow was still distraught over Isaac Rosenfeld's death that summer; he would later write a poignant, troubled memoir of Rosenfeld in short story form, "Zetland: By a Character Witness." (He had planned for "Zetland" to be a whole book, but he never finished it; the loss was too close.) At that lunch Bellow gave Ellison a copy of his new book, *Seize the Day*, and invited him to share the house he had just bought with a small inheritance from his father.

"We've bought ourselves a wreck of a house in Tivoli

(New York)," Bellow wrote to Ellison earlier in 1956. The three-story run-down Italianate villa in the Hudson Valley hamlet, near Bard College, would be immortalized in Bellow's *Herzog.* Perched on a hilltop with a fine view of verdant countryside, it was impossible to heat because of its floor-to-ceiling windows. The floorboards drooped and cratered, and cracked paint peeled off the walls. The grand ballroom was falling to pieces. There was little water, so Bellow dug a well. During the summer of 1956, the novelist, who sardonically called his manse "Bellowview," spent much of his time painting, sanding, digging, weeding the garden, and trying to fix the plumbing, while Sondra was pregnant with Adam, Bellow's second son.

Greg Bellow, then twelve years old, was there for much of that first summer in Tivoli, along with Rosenfeld's widow, Vasiliki. There were plenty of bedrooms, all of them in bad repair. Two years later, in late summer 1958, Ellison moved into the Tivoli house and began teaching at Bard. Ellison's wife, Fanny, arrived on Friday evening and went back to the city on Sunday afternoon. Bellow and Ellison together applied themselves to gardening. In time the Tivoli garden would become a source of pride for Bellow: Rosette Lamont, later a Bellow girlfriend, remembers him crowing, "Look at my tomatoes, they're the size of dinosaur's balls."

At the end of the fifties Bellow was teaching at the University of Minnesota, another short-term gig for the gypsy novelist. He came back to stay in Tivoli for the summers of 1959 and 1960. The first summer, the Bellows shared the vast, rambling mansion with Ralph and Fanny. The second summer, Bellow came alone: his marriage had dissolved in June 1960 amid Sondra's ferocious recriminations, followed by Bellow's discovery that Sondra had been having an affair with his sycophantic friend Jack Ludwig. Bellow would provide his own marital therapy in *Herzog*, where he caricatured both Sondra and Jack in high, raging style.

Bellow, who had taught at Bard earlier in the fifties, described the college in a letter to his fellow faculty member Ted Weiss as a "*pays de merveilles*, cloud-cuckoo, monkey-on-the-back, avant-garde booby cosmos." Bard was a bastion of scruffy young bohemians, prep-school outcasts, and seekers. Ellison complained in a letter that the Bard students "wear beards and let their unwashed tits bounce around in their low-cut blouses and are still, literally, chewing gum." (Ellison himself was always a fastidious dresser.) But he seems to have been popular with the students, a charismatic, hardworking teacher who led them through Conrad, Stephen Crane, Dostoevsky, and Faulkner.

Bard was at times a rocky experience for Ellison. He once so angered a faculty wife from Arkansas that she called him a nigger. (Ellison kept his cool and, without skipping a beat, said to her, "Kiss me.") Gore Vidal, who lived nearby, is said to have asked Ellison, "What's a jungle bunny like you doing in these parts?" When Ellison and Bellow later came to dinner at Vidal's home, Ellison had his revenge. After sitting through one of Vidal's fervent sermons against American imperialism, Ellison blandly remarked, "Gore, I just don't understand your problem with this country. You rich, you white, and you pretty. What've you got to complain about?"

In Tivoli Bellow charged Ellison no rent, and paid for utilities and expenses as well. "I get a few hundred dollars a year from my father's estate which just about covers the fuel costs," he wrote Ellison from Minneapolis. He knew that Ellison was suffering from both marital and creative worries (Fanny had found out about Ellison's Rome affair), and he did what he could to help.

The cure worked, at least in part. Ellison at the Tivoli mansion was "like a nineteenth century Englishman living in Africa," he wrote to Albert Murray. He hunted rabbits and ducks, sipped wine by the fire, read and cooked, and tended to his African violets, which he watered with a turkey baster.

"As writers are natural solitaries, Ralph and I did not seek each other out during the day," Bellow remembered about life at Tivoli. In the morning Ellison came down to breakfast in a djellaba and pointed-toe Persian slippers and made coffee in his expert manner. He then went to the study he had set up in the ballroom, while Bellow stayed at his own desk, where he listened to Mozart operas and wrote feverishly. Bellow and Ellison had breakfast and dinner together almost every day.

Ellison, coming off the mammoth success of *Invisible Man*, still had "a writer's block as big as the Ritz," as he put it. But he spent long hours each day at the typewriter, as he would throughout his life. By the time Ellison died, he had amassed thousands of pages of his unfinished second novel, a work that, he often promised his eager readership, was all but ready for publication. But the manuscript remained a chaos, encrusted with labyrinthine digressions. Bellow blamed Ellison's friend Stanley Edgar Hyman, the critic who had advised him on the drafts of *Invisible Man*; he said that Hyman had "encouraged Ralph to be ponderous." Ellison should have been more like his slippery con artist Rinehart in *Invisible Man*, vanished from the scene before you could blink twice. Or, as you might say in Yiddish, *neylm gevorn*.

Ellison's second novel would become a massive tangle, wild and ungoverned. In the end, after four decades of work, he never finished the book. (Ellison's literary executor, John Callahan, eventually edited two volumes of selections from Ellison's manuscript, *Juneteenth* and *Three Days Before the Shooting*.) In his reminiscence of their time together, Bellow voiced his admiration for Ellison's "powers of organization": when going on a trip, Ellison would beautifully arrange the car trunk, with water, blanket, suitcase, flashlight, and tools all in place. Bellow didn't have to add that, in the arena of writing, Ellison's organizational powers were failing him.

"Ralph had the bearing of a distinguished man," Bellow wrote later about Ellison in Tivoli: an aristocratic posture, native independence, and courage. Ellison for his part was deeply amused at Bellow's lack of sartorial class, his jeans and torn T-shirts. (After living with Ellison, Bellow would become a self-consciously dapper dresser.) At cocktail hour Ellison talked to Bellow about his youth in Oklahoma and about American history, a subject he knew much better than Bellow. He was, Bellow sensed, going over the facts of his own life so he could join them together with the collective story of black America. But in his manuscript Ellison's memories would become recursive, clotted. Bellow by contrast was moving in the direction of *Herzog*, which takes the dark obsessive meditations of a betrayed husband and makes them agile and comic. Bellow was achieving lightness in his art; Ellison's writing had begun to turn slow and heavy.

Tuckatarby, Ellison's puppy, was the snake in the Eden that was Tivoli. Tucka chewed books and defecated in the herb garden and on the Persian rugs. Bellow loudly objected, but the childless Ellison cherished his dog: in his eyes Tucka could do no wrong. Ellison complained to John Cheever, who lived nearby, that Bellow, having grown up with mongrels, was unused to the habits of a purebred dog. In a few years' time, Ellison would choose Cheever over Bellow. Always a hard fighter on awards committees, Ellison battled strenuously in 1965 to award the Howells Medal for Fiction to Cheever's *The Wapshot Scandal* instead of *Herzog*. He won the fight, and Cheever reported himself embarrassed that "Ralph wouldn't let them give the thing to Saul."

It's not clear what, besides the bad behavior of Tucka, broke up the companionship between Bellow and Ellison. After Bellow moved to Chicago in 1961 and married his third wife, Susan Glassman, his meetings and exchanges of letters with Ellison dwindled to almost nothing. Ellison's heavy drinking must have played a significant role: for Bellow alcohol was a *goyishe* affliction for which he had little sympathy. It may be too that both Ellison and Bellow recognized the growing gap between them. Ellison, the stalled novelist, was becoming a spokesman on the racial crisis in America. His independent-minded liberal stance let him keep his distance from Black Power and the New Left. He liked LBJ, who had him to dinner more than a few times, and unlike nearly all of his fellow writers, supported the Vietnam War. Bellow, in contrast to the post–*Invisible Man* Ellison, spoke to and about his era through his novels.

Bellow the Jew could avoid becoming a political and cultural spokesman as Ellison the African American could not. Ellison wrote in a 1953 essay that "the Negro stereotype is really an image of the unorganized, irrational forces of American life." To combat that stereotype was the inevitable role for Ellison; there was no escape. Bellow was free to declare, as he did more than once, that he was really an American rather than a Jewish writer. Being black in America was not and is not like being Jewish in America.

When Bellow considered chaos and irrational forces, he thought not about race but the rampant emotional battles that made his marriages collapse. "He was always making and breaking families," Bellow's son Adam says. His repeated marital catastrophes seemed to Bellow to be happening to him, events rather than acts of will on his part. Yet he decided to leave Anita; he made the disastrous choice of Sondra, and then, after his second marriage caved in, he picked a third bride uncannily similar to Sondra, Susan Glassman. Bellow's two novels of the late fifties, *Seize the Day* and *Henderson the Rain King*, are both about men who have made a staggering mess of their lives. Bellow was waxing autobiographical.

In the summer of 1956, *Partisan Review* published *Seize the Day*, a pure, efficient, small masterpiece. Its hero is a trapped, hopeless loser, and Bellow feels for his case as he does for his own. The powerfully concentrated *Seize the Day* looks back to a taut noir style: if we didn't know better we might guess that it belongs to the thirties or forties rather than the mid-fifties. Bellow's hero, Tommy Wilhelm, lives in the narrow straits of debt and discouragement, persecuted by a harsh, business-minded father and tempted by a con artist named Tamkin. In Tamkin Bellow produced his only portrait of a smoothly fraudulent, wizardlike seducer; at times he appears to have come straight out of Iris Murdoch. Tamkin's monologues hypnotize the reader of *Seize the Day* just as they do the hapless Tommy. He also resembles one of *Invisible Man*'s fluent, crooked mentors, a Bledsoe ready to lead the young narrator astray. *Seize the Day* is the only novel by Bellow that is not at all about women. Like Ellison, he focuses on the father figures who keep you running, who either refuse to provide or else provide the wrong thing.

Tommy Wilhelm is a sweating, slowly desperate middle-aged man: short of money, separated from his wife and kids, with no visible prospects in life. Tommy reflects Bellow's own fearful self-image in the mid-fifties, the feeling of stymied failure reinforced by his brother Morrie's disdain. In *Seize the Day* Tommy begs for money from his father, who lives in the same Upper West Side hotel that he does, and the father bluntly refuses. The fraught relation between father and son springs from Bellow's own sense that he had disappointed the recently dead Abraham by becoming a hand-to-mouth novelist rather than a businessman. "There's no need to carry on like an opera, Wilky," his father, Dr. Adler, tells him (Tommy used to be Wilky Adler; he has changed both his first and his last name). "This is only your side of things." And again: "'I don't understand your problems,' said the old man. 'I never had any like them.'" Dr. Adler, cool and by the book, is ready to calmly wash his hands of a good-for-nothing son, not at all like Bellow's own violent-tempered father. But Abraham Bellow had the same readiness to turn his back on his sons: he regularly warned them that they might be cut out of his will.

Bellow finished *Seize the Day* in the Hudson Valley, but it is a New York City book. A noirish flourish appears on its very first page. Tommy is walking through the lobby of the hotel where he lives: "In the blue air Tommy saw a pigeon about to light on the great chain that supported the marquee of the movie house directly underneath the lobby. For one moment he heard the wings beating strongly."

With this dour portent supplied by that typical New York beast, the pigeon, Bellow glances at time's iron-winged chariot. Tommy's character is his fate, and he changes very little from first to last: he is as static as any hard-boiled pulp hero. *Seize the Day*, a controlled story of repression and quiet defeat, draws on the American noir tradition but without its macho sternness. The book's conclusion is not austere but instead flowing, passionate, and grave, as Tommy Wilhelm weeps for his own life at the funeral of a stranger.

Bellow's own favorite character in *Seize the Day* was Tamkin, the memorable confidence man who recites his half-literate inspirational verse to the bewildered Tommy. Tamkin is a slick and genuinely strange man, a false father ready to replace Tommy's real one. Tamkin bets on the commodities market, and he gets Tommy to invest with him in lard futures. The outcome is disastrous—Tommy loses his shirt. A consummate flimflam man, Tamkin trumpets fake-Emersonian self-reliance ("You should try some of my 'here-and-now' mental exercises," he says to Tommy). Mintouchian's inspired talk in *Augie March* has become advice for suckers. But astoundingly Tamkin speaks truth as well. He condemns the "pretender soul" that, he says, obeys the "society mechanism"; the pretender is in a duel to the death with the buried "true soul." "I hear them, poor human beasts. I can't help hearing," Tamkin laments. "And my eyes are open to it. I have to cry, too. This is the human tragedy-comedy." "How can he be such a jerk," Tommy asks himself, "and even perhaps an operator, a swindler, and understand so well what gives?"

The crooked Tamkin is in fact a psychoanalyst of the hidden life. When he asks Tommy, "You love your old man?" Tommy stammers an answer, and Bellow gives a superbly tense image for his hero's undercover emotion:

> Wilhelm grasped at this. "Of course, of course I love him. My father. My mother—" As he said this there was a great pull at the very center of his soul. When a fish strikes the line you feel the live force in your

> hand. A mysterious being beneath the water, driven by hunger, has taken the hook and rushes away and fights, writhing. Wilhelm never identified what struck within him. It did not reveal itself. It got away.

The tight-lipped repression signaled by the fish that got away does not satisfy in the end. Bellow and his hero need catharsis.

Passion comes out in the book's last scene, when Tommy weeps at the funeral and sinks "deeper than sorrow, through torn sobs and cries toward the consummation of the heart's ultimate need." Bellow gives us a Wagnerian *Liebestod*, with grief rather than love sounding "the great and happy oblivion of tears." Bellow was clearly remembering the end of Joyce's "The Dead," but he drives the hero's emotion much harder than Joyce does.

At his father's funeral in 1955, Bellow wept uncontrollably, much as Tommy Wilhelm does at the end of *Seize the Day*. Morrie told him angrily, "Don't carry on like an immigrant." (Morrie wasn't alone: Philip Roth complained in print about the "schmaltzed-up" ending of *Seize the Day*.)

The jaws close on Tommy Wilhelm, and his mistakes add up to disaster. There is no room for an enlarged self, no appetite for more life such as we see in Augie, Henderson, Humboldt, Ravelstein and even Herzog. In *Seize the Day* Bellow turns his spotlight on the constricted mood of the fifties in America. Tommy's father provides an insidious guilt-tripping, intended to smother or erase his son, which was also present in Bellow's first two novels. It appears that

Abraham's death returned Bellow, the mourning son, to the anxious, airless world of his first two books. His next novel, the rip-roaring *Henderson the Rain King*, would leave that world forever behind.

Tommy Wilhelm of *Seize the Day* is Bellow's purest image of failure in his work. While Bellow was writing the book, he knew Ellison was in profound trouble both as a writer and as a husband. I have already mentioned that at the lunch in 1956 when he gave Ellison his copy of the just published *Seize the Day*, Bellow invited Ellison to live with him and Sondra in Tivoli. He wanted to rescue Ellison from Tommy's fate.

There was another friend who would never be rescued—Isaac Rosenfeld, who died just after *Seize the Day* came out. Bellow had been thinking of Isaac too when he created Tommy Wilhelm, his most trapped and hopeless protagonist.

In an August 1956 letter to Gertrude Buckman, Delmore Schwartz's first wife, Bellow said he had been "thrown millions of light years by Isaac Rosenfeld's death" earlier that summer, and to John Berryman he wrote in December, "I think and think about Isaac, and my recollections are endless—twenty-six years, of which I've forgotten very little." For a time Ellison in Tivoli substituted for Bellow's dead friend, but he could never rival Isaac in Bellow's memory.

Like Ellison, Rosenfeld became a brilliant failure in Bellow's eyes. He tried hard to escape the prison of respectability that loomed over his friend Bellow. Isaac was another shadow self for Bellow, like Morrie, like Ralph.

CHAPTER 3

Isaac Rosenfeld and Chanler Chapman

IN HIS FOREWORD to a collection of Isaac Rosenfeld's essays, *An Age of Enormity*, Bellow described his boyhood friend, dead at the age of thirty-eight:

> Isaac had a round face and yellowish-brown hair which he combed straight back. He was nearsighted, his eyes pale blue, and he wore round glasses. The space between his large teeth gave his smile an ingenuous charm. He had a belly laugh. It came on him abruptly and often doubled him up. His smiles, however, kindled slowly. He liked to look with avuncular owlishness over the tops of his specs. His wisecracks were often preceded by the pale blue glance. He began, he paused, a sort of mild slyness formed about his lips, and then he said something devastating. More seriously, developing an argu-

> ment, he gestured like a Russian-Jewish intellectual, a cigarette between two fingers. When he was in real earnest, he put aside these mannerisms, too. A look of strength, sometimes of angry strength, came into his eyes.

For Bellow, as for many others, Rosenfeld was an irresistible presence, a Yiddish Puck or Cherubino, the winning, mischievous child-man. Rosenfeld stayed with Bellow all the way through their youth, from Tuley High School to the University of Chicago to the University of Wisconsin, where Bellow studied anthropology and Rosenfeld philosophy. (Before Wisconsin, Bellow completed his undergraduate degree at Northwestern; Rosenfeld remained at Chicago.) They both moved to New York around the same time: Rosenfeld came in 1941; Bellow, after a number of trips to the city during the war years, arrived with Anita and Greg in 1945.

When they were boys together in Chicago, Bellow and Rosenfeld were nicknamed Kamenev and Zinoviev, after the Soviet Jewish commissars. A rumor was even going around Madison that Isaac was Trotsky's nephew; Isaac had started it himself, as a joke, but people began to believe it. Isaac adored the fierce dishevelment of Russian passion, which he saw as very close to the Jewish style. He once jokingly suggested that Chekhov actually wrote in Yiddish, but that this fact had been concealed to make him more universally appealing. In New York in the forties, Bellow,

Rosenfeld, and Oscar Tarcov, another Tuley High School pal, were known as "the Chicago Dostoevskyans."

Rosenfeld's own fiction was not turbulently Russian in temper but rather dreamy and gentle. His novel *Passage from Home*, published in 1946 when Rosenfeld was twenty-eight, received rapturous reviews from the New York intelligentsia, including Diana Trilling, a very tough critic. The book was tender and Proustian, told through the eyes of a small boy, befitting Rosenfeld's image as the perpetual child. In its opening pages the fourteen-year-old narrator gets drunk on one too many cups of wine at a Passover seder. He has the otherworldly privilege of boyhood, which Rosenfeld himself clung to throughout his life.

Rosenfeld's own dreaminess, his luftmensch nature, was a reaction against his father, who pushed him to be an overachiever, a little boy genius. Bellow described Sam Rosenfeld in "Zetland," his fictional portrait of Isaac, as "white-jowled, a sarcastic bear." Sam was easily wounded, and authoritarian when offended. Behind his back his son called him the General or the Commissar. Isaac played the flute and read Kant, obedient to his father's wish that he should pursue music and high culture. He felt stunted, a deformed prodigy. Throughout his short life Rosenfeld yearned after the pure, untroubled childhood he never had. At Rosenfeld's core, writes his biographer Steven Zipperstein, was an "emotional hunger incapable of being sated."

Bellow adored Rosenfeld but also scorned his innocence. Bellow suggested in "Zetland" that Isaac was "virtually a Franciscan, a simpleton for God's sake, easy to cheat." Isaac did play the holy fool at times. In one letter to Tarcov, from November 1941, Isaac wrote, "I will say to you and to Saul, and to every body, believe in God. That means believe, have faith in yourselves, love, be cheerful. . . . Paste it on Saul's forehead, paste it on your own."

In a comic piece he wrote for the college newspaper when they were U. of C. undergraduates, Isaac called Bellow Raskolnikov, while he described himself as "simper[ing] self-consciously." Bellow played the role of ruthless Morrie, while Rosenfeld was the young Saul being wised up by his more worldly older brother. Bellow wrote to Tarcov in September 1937 about "the renaissance of Isaac," who, thanks to Bellow, was "beginning to spring a little gristle in his marrow. Who knows, he may develop bone if he continues."

Rosenfeld was a hopped-up performer, a card. When he and Bellow were at the University of Chicago, they performed surreal comic sketches in the library ("foaming rabbis rub electrical fish") and composed together a famous Yiddish parody of Eliot's Prufrock (a sample: *"ikh ver alt, ikh ver alt, / Un di pupik vert mir kalt"*: "I grow old, I grow old, / And my belly-button is getting cold"). In "Zetland" the Rosenfeld character walks down the street practicing string quartets: he "made the violin stops inside his fuzz-lined gloves and puffed the music in his throat and cheeks. . . . He did the cello in his chest and the violins high in the nose." He is Bellow's version of Rameau's nephew, a freak of nature with a happy talent for imitation and parody.

Rosenfeld was a talented humorist. Zipperstein cites a letter that Rosenfeld wrote to his high school girlfriend Freda Davis (who returned to him shortly before his death, after his marriage had broken up). In the letter, Rosenfeld defines matzoh as

> An old Roman article of diet introduced into Roman life by POMPEIUS ATTLATICUS MANISHEWITZ in the year 57 B.C. The Romans used Matzoh for fuel, they built barricades and bridges out of it. Many of the bridges built by the early Romans out of Matzoh are still standing. Matzoh was also widely used as food and it formed the chief article of diet among invalids, prisoners, imbeciles, and Senators. The Roman Matrons of the Patrician Class found it indispensable to the instruction of their young daughters.

Isaac's passion for Freda was like Bellow's for Eleanor Fox, a rapturous first love that both men dwelt on later with intense nostalgia. "'Yet there lives the dearest freshness deep down things'—Freda," Rosenfeld wrote in his journal. But Isaac, like Bellow, moved on romantically. In 1940, in Chicago, Isaac met Vasiliki Sarantakis, a petite "pagan beauty" with a wild streak and "Harpo Marx hair." "She wears earrings, looks Jewish, acts crazy, and I think the world of her," Isaac wrote to Oscar Tarcov. He added that "she is quite easygoing, hedonistic to a fault, at the exclusion of certain moral, intellectual and metaphysical values." Isaac wanted the hedonism; he saw in it a promise of freedom.

In another letter to Tarcov, from March 1941, Isaac voiced his misgivings about studying philosophy. Melville and Whitman sparked him: "I have been reading *Moby-Dick* (Have you read it?)," he wrote:

> It is a magnificent book, devil brewed, metaphysical and compassionate. Between *Moby-Dick* and *Leaves of Grass*, and a few other books, so full of soul, may I some day discover them all, there is enough to make all philosophy stemming from the U. of C. ridiculous.

Rosenfeld recounted that the previous night, after reading Whitman, "It grew late, and I had to return to my paper. There it lay, curled in the typewriter, a nice long neat list of definitions and postulates. I broke out laughing!"

Despite his doubts about the field, Rosenfeld accepted a fellowship to study philosophy at New York University, beginning in the fall of 1941. Isaac and Vasiliki shared a disorderly lifestyle in New York: an open marriage in a series of cramped, dirty apartments. At first they lived on the Upper West Side, with their bathtub in the kitchen and cockroaches leaping from the toaster. Later, they moved to the Village, the city's teeming, unkempt intellectual and artistic center.

Before the end of his first year at NYU, Rosenfeld dropped out of school and started to make his way as a writer, while Vasiliki worked as a secretary to bring home the money. He started with the trade journal *Ice Cream World*, but quickly moved up. Rosenfeld's essays and stories began to come out in *Partisan Review*, the place that counted most, and he reviewed books for the *New Republic*. "It was still a shame and a disgrace to work for the *New Republic*—because they had defended the Moscow trials," Rosenfeld's friend David Bazelon recalled in an essay.

"Isaac was my friend from the time we were boys," Bellow said in a 1984 interview. "He became successful in New York when he was young and fresh from Chicago, as a reviewer and essayist. He was in a lot of the journals and magazines and was doing very well. But then he went through analysis with someone following the program of Reich." Wilhelm Reich, whose influence on Bellow I have already mentioned, was most famous for his invention of the orgone box, a container in which one was supposed to sit naked and absorb orgone energy. The goal was to achieve total orgasm, a sexual fulfillment that would release the self from its lockstep adherence to society's norms, the conventions that clamp us down and rob us of erotic and spiritual wholeness.

For all the crankish lunacy of his later career, which was replete with bizarre inventions like the cloud-buster (a rainmaking device), Reich was a serious thinker. With his Weimar toughness, he judged that liberalism had shown itself a patent failure, whereas fascism had succeeded in harnessing the primitive energies deep within human beings. Reich, the Austrian-Jewish refugee from the Nazis, would compete with fascism for the human soul. Fascism was authoritarian through and through; Reich wanted to crush the authoritarian strain that runs so deep in us. His patients screamed, raged, acted out their craziest passions so that they could be free.

Reichian therapy was sometimes brutal: the analyst vigorously massaged patients to release them from deadening "character armor." The patient's defenses had to be broken down through verbal attack so that he could be freed from his rigid day-to-day character. In "Charm and Death," an unpublished Bellow manuscript, the Rosenfeld character gets abused by his Reichian therapist, and not just verbally: he comes out of the office covered in bruises.

Isaac, Bellow remembered in his 1984 interview, "became a fanatical Reichian," and even "applied Reich to the raising of his children. He built an orgone box. Finally he became a kind of Dostoyevskian clown. He was ruined by this stuff. He got a divorce and was leading a radical sex life. It had a terrible effect, and finally his life on Barrow Street just blew up." Bellow added, "I didn't want to lose him when all that was happening. So I went through the analysis too, just to stay close. It was very difficult. You know, I think Isaac thought I was a patsy for sentimentality and that Freud and Reich would make one hard."

Even though he sometimes spoke of his Reichian therapy as just an effort to be loyal to Isaac, Bellow's long commitment to Reichian ideas was a major part of his life. He knew he was a rigid, nervous man, often competitive and vain, carrying on unsatisfying affairs with women.

His character armor was thick, encrusted. Part of Bellow wanted liberation, a breakthrough into Reichian orgasmic fulfillment. But he could never be liberation-minded in the way that Rosenfeld was. Rosenfeld made himself vulnerable with his open marriage to Vasiliki—an unthinkable arrangement for Bellow, who was incapable by nature of Isaac's unruly bohemianism. Yet he admired, he loved, Rosenfeld's boldness.

Not just Rosenfeld's chaotic sexuality but his other drastic life choices show him to be, unlike Bellow, daring and incautious. In 1944 he quit a job as assistant literary editor of the *New Republic* to work for a few months on a barge in New York harbor. Rosenfeld was an incendiary writer, too, at least once. His essay "Adam and Eve on Delancey Street," published in 1949 in *Commentary*, caused a scandal. Rosenfeld described an eager crowd watching "kosher fry beef," a Jewish substitute for bacon, being cooked at a store on New York's Lower East Side. Salivating at the sight of so much delectable meat, the crowd lines up for egg creams instead. Rosenfeld went on to speculate that kosher dietary law has its roots in sexual taboo: to mix milk and meat is to dangerously mingle female and male. Kashrut, Rosenfeld claimed, perfectly expresses the sexual repression so central to the orthodox Jewish household. The article provoked outrage from some respectable Jewish quarters, and the well-known rabbi and author Milton Steinberg campaigned vigorously against Rosenfeld. All told, the affair enhanced Rosenfeld's brave bohemian reputation.

Rosenfeld, the pudgy, round-faced, and bespectacled

prodigy, was the eternal boy. His happy animation made those around him feel free. Irving Howe remembered his "air of yeshiva purity" and added, "Isaac made me feel the world is spacious." But in his thirties Rosenfeld himself was feeling trapped and melancholic. He was separated, on and off, from Vasiliki and their two children. In his letters and journals, gaiety alternated with despair. He wrote to Tarcov in April 1951 that "I feel much more alive and younger than I've been in years. . . . Underneath it all, there's still a certain desperateness, but I hope it will pass." Two years later, again to Tarcov, he lamented, "I feel 500,000 years older. The prolonged crisis of the last 18 months has taken that much out of me. I've decided to try it with Vasiliki and the kids again. Wish us well."

Rosenfeld wrote in one of his notebooks, "I have attacks of hatefulness during which I can see only the evil in others and am overcome by fear. At such times I think all men are unconscious murderers." But, he added, "out of this hatred and panic fear, I must release my love for men and women." Rosenfeld filled pages in his journal with Freudian analyses of *Crime and Punishment*. He wanted to break free of his guilt the way Dostoevsky's murderer does at the end of the novel. But he never found liberation.

In October 1955, close to the end (Rosenfeld died in July 1956), he wrote, "It's awful, being alone in Chicago." In his desperate last journal, Isaac laments that he cannot love Vasiliki and asks, "Maybe I have learned something? That I have been wrong for the last 7–9 years. One does not, must not live by or for passions alone: that a life of such a kind is destructive?"

Rosenfeld wound up dying alone, in a rented room in Chicago—the kind of dingy place, one of Rosenfeld's friends said, where you could imagine Raskolnikov sharpening his axe. Bellow wrote in his *Partisan Review* obituary for his friend, "He died in a seedy, furnished room on Walton Street, alone—a bitter death to his children, his wife, his lovers, his father."

When he was an undergraduate at Chicago, Rosenfeld had performed with the Compass Players, a student troupe that included Mike Nichols, Elaine May, and Shelly Berman. One of his skits was peeling an onion with intense silent concentration, only to discover nothing at the center. A tour de force of comedy that ends in baffled frustration: such was Rosenfeld's own tragic course.

"Zetland" has a unique ending for a Bellow story: it concludes with an elated wish fulfillment. Astonished by his reading of *Moby-Dick*, Zetland quits NYU with heartfelt support from Lottie, the Vasiliki character. The story concludes, "Lottie was always for him, and she supported him against his father, who of course disapproved." Bellow airbrushes out of his story the heated quarrels between Isaac and Vasiliki, along with the fact that their marriage cracked up. To have published more of "Charm and Death" would have been to show Rosenfeld as a victim, Bellow knew, and perhaps also as an unpleasant manipulator at times (the way he appears in Wallace Markfield's novel *To an Early Grave*, the basis for Sidney Lumet's 1968 movie *Bye Bye Braverman*). He needed Isaac to remain pure, an innocent to the end.

Rosenfeld also wrote about Bellow, in veiled form. In his short story "King Solomon," the Israelite monarch is transparently Bellow, transformed into a fat, pinochle-playing old man who can still attract women. The story is a slow-moving, pomp-dusted fable, full of creaky oriental trappings and heavily suggesting Rosenfeld's envy of his more successful friend.

Bellow had an intense sense of guilt about Rosenfeld's failures and his own triumphs. "I loved him, but we were rivals," he wrote in a 1956 letter. Bellow admits that he was sometimes "insufferable, and not at all a constant friend." ("I was naughty with Saul," Vasiliki confessed to a mutual friend.)

In March 1952, Bellow wrote Tarcov that he was "tired of being envied or grudged every bit of success or imagined success," and complained about Isaac's "not too well hidden hope that I fall on my face." Later, Bellow felt guilty over his success with *Augie March*, while Rosenfeld expressed his disappointment with Bellow's novel. Rosenfeld remarked to the writer and editor Monroe Engel in the fifties, "Someday Saul or I will win the Nobel Prize." When Bellow won the Nobel, decades after Rosenfeld's death, he is reported to have said, "It should have been Isaac."

Bellow's *Henderson the Rain King*, the novel he completed shortly after Rosenfeld's death, was both a reaching out to Isaac and a way of getting beyond him. In a nod to Rosenfeld's "King Solomon," Isaac appears as the African King Dahfu. But the hero, Eugene Henderson, was based on Chanler Chapman, Bellow's landlord and friend while he was teaching at Bard. Bellow discovered in Chapman the antidote to Isaac's powerful lingering presence. Chapman lived in the present with gusto, never plagued by the shadows of failure that clung to Rosenfeld.

"THERE ARE TIMES when I must, and literally do, howl," Bellow wrote to Henry Volkening, his literary agent, about his Reichian exercises in 1956, when he was going out behind his cottage in Reno and shouting into the desert air. *Henderson* is one long howl, an outburst, a letting go. "The worse my personal disasters became," Bellow said, "the funnier *Henderson* seemed to get."

Henderson is an adventure story about an American traveling to the other side of the world—deepest, darkest Africa—in an effort to find reality, meaning, and self-knowledge: in short, all the therapeutic big ideas of the fifties (and now), ideas that Bellow burlesques in his novel but also takes seriously. He plays existential anxiety for laughs, yet we are also drawn by Henderson's quest. There is nothing somber about Bellow the author of *Henderson*, unlike the European modernists and existentialists who had impressed Americans with their high sobriety—and unlike Bellow himself in *Seize the Day*. In *Henderson*, Bellow proves that an American *Heart of Darkness* will look very different from its Conradian precursor: strong and lusty, absentminded and sometimes cloddish, full of crazy light and self-pleased guffaws.

Where is authenticity to be found? Bellow asked in *Henderson*, and implied that the New York intellectuals, with their love of high modernism, were looking for it in the wrong place. The authentic is not at the bottom of the abyss with Conrad's sublime-solemn Kurtz. Bellow's stance has nothing in common with those of Beckett or Kafka. He turns decisively away from the modernist cult of being in extremis that Rosenfeld, like most of the *Partisan Review* writers, had taken so seriously. Bellow is instead a comic novelist, looking for freedom anywhere he can find it. Eugene Henderson becomes Bellow's brawny exemplar of personality: ready, even eager, to make any mistake in the hope of answering the unruly open question that is his life.

Henderson was also Bellow's first WASP hero, and he broke the usual mold of such characters in fifties fiction. Henderson's midlife crisis comes out with garrulous and unembarrassed frankness, rather than in the poignant, yearning manner of John Cheever's alienated suburbanites or John Updike's Rabbit (*Rabbit, Run* came out in 1960, the year after *Henderson*).

The clownlike Henderson, a physical giant with great stamina, is large in feeling, passionately frustrated. He is as unflappable as Don Quixote, able to shrug off his failures and plow ahead. Henderson leaves his wife and children in Connecticut—"Christ, I've got plenty of kids"—and takes a brave and aimless trip to Africa. He wants to get as far away as he can from everything he knows. Henderson is fifty-five, about ten years older than his author, and is recklessly determined to bash his head against reality, willy-nilly—to see what's out there, and what better place than Africa?

Years later, Bellow would visit Kenya with his Henderson-like friend Dave Peltz, who was considering putting money into some beryllium mines. On the streets of Nairobi, by pure chance, Bellow ran into the artist Saul Steinberg. Bellow and Steinberg then took a river cruise together and were gaped at by a hungry crocodile, whereupon the novelist imagined a fitting news headline: "Crocodile Eats Two Sauls." This was as close as Bellow ever came to a harrowing African adventure. He made up *Henderson* out of whole cloth, though he took some snippets from Sir Richard Burton and other storied travelers. Bellow's old anthropology teacher at Northwestern, Melville Herskovits, didn't approve: Africa was too serious a subject for a writer to be inventing tribal names and customs, he said. Bellow had clearly drawn on H. Rider Haggard and Burton as well as anthropology—in one letter he asked a friend to find for him a copy of Burton's *A Mission to Gelele, King of Dahome*, since "I need it for some of the details."

"In my own way, I worked very hard. Violent suffering is labor, and frequently I was drunk before lunch," Henderson marvelously says about his life before Africa. Well over six feet and two hundred pounds, Henderson has the strength of a linebacker but remains, at bottom, a big child. He avoids both alcohol and sex during his time in Africa. The huge homunculus Henderson, a shy, polite fellow for all his bluster, resembles the Odysseus who shrinks before Nausicaa. He lacks, however, Odysseus's skill at diplomacy. He hears a voice inside him calling, "*I want, I want, I want!*"—but what he wants, he doesn't begin to know.

Henderson gives us a loud, moaning catalogue on the book's first page: "The facts begin to crowd me and soon I get a pressure in the chest. A disorderly rush begins—my parents, my wives, my girls, my children, my farm, my animals, my habits, my money, my music lessons, my drunkenness, my prejudices, my brutality, my teeth, my face, my soul!" Rosenfeld had that same pressure in the chest, the same sharp sense that his life was a mountain of grief. Despite his Reichian practices, he could never find the release that Henderson discovers on his African trip.

Not every reader will love Henderson, self-centered buffo that he is. "Why should I care about this guy?" asked my wife when I showed her the first page of the book. "He's an asshole." Yet Henderson exists in a world of his own, head, heart, and soul—like Don Quixote, who can be just as bullish and brutal. He exults in harsh reality even when it rubs him raw. "When I was in the Army and caught the crabs," he says, his fellow soldiers washed him, shaved him naked, and left him "bald and shivering," "prickling between the legs and under the arms, raging, laughing, and swearing revenge." Henderson remembers "that beautiful sky, and the mad itch and the razors; and the Mediterranean, which is the cradle of mankind; the towering softness of the air; the sinking softness of the water, where Ulysses got lost, where he, too, was naked as the sirens sang." This hearty yet lyrical barracks humor plops us back in the world of the Spanish picaresque novel *Lazarillo de Tormes*, of Smollett, and of Fielding. The gross bodily satire is that of an overgrown boy who delights in health and who hears the song of wind, water, and sky.

Henderson finds a mentor during his African trip: Dahfu, ruler of the Wariri tribe (invented by Bellow). Dahfu has captured a lioness that becomes his spiritual companion. The king cavorts with and caresses the beast, and even clings to her belly for a ride around the perimeter of her cell. He teaches the terrified Henderson to conquer his fear of the lioness, to play with her as he would a cat.

Bellow's son Greg, in his moving memoir of his father, argues convincingly that Dahfu represents Rosenfeld, Bellow's risk-taking alter ego. Critics have noticed that Dahfu sounds like a Reichian therapist, expounding ideas about breathing and physiognomy similar to Reich's. Bellow first encountered Reich through Rosenfeld, Reich's truest disciple among their circle of friends. The proud African king was Bellow's idealized image of what Rosenfeld longed for but could never achieve, a brave freedom.

Dahfu says to Henderson, speaking of the gifts the lioness will bring him, "Oh, you have accomplished momentous avoidances. But she will change that. She will make consciousness to shine. She will burnish you. She will force the present moment upon you." Dahfu tasks Henderson with opening himself up to the present, something that the habitually cagey and cautious Bellow could never do. Like the lost Rosenfeld, Dahfu sees into Henderson's core.

Dahfu will eventually be killed by a lion during a hunt. Henderson becomes a helpless spectator to the tragedy of

Dahfu, which he can do nothing to prevent; he has been so absorbed in his own quest for selfhood that he becomes useless to Dahfu. There is an autobiographical message here: *Henderson* reads like a critique of the way Bellow's own personal struggles eclipsed his duty to his closest friend.

Praised be rashness is Dahfu's lesson—in this he echoes the rash Rosenfeld—and there is something rash in the mighty undirected gusto of Bellow's novel. The book ends with Henderson headed back home, on an airplane that has stopped in Newfoundland for refueling. On the flight he cuddles a Persian orphan in his arms, and he also has with him, outlandishly, a lion cub from Africa. Now he takes eager laps around the Newfoundland ice, with the plane gleaming above him. Bellow seems to have forgotten that Henderson is returning to his wife and children, the family he has given so little thought to during his travels. The end of the novel avoids the question that Bellow himself was dodging in the late fifties, when his marriage to Sondra broke apart: How strong are the ties to wife and child measured against the need for lone adventure and self-discovery?

BELLOW LOVINGLY ECHOED Rosenfeld in his portrait of King Dahfu, but, as I have mentioned, he based his hero Henderson on Chanler Chapman, his roughneck aristocrat neighbor and onetime landlord in Barrytown, New York. The two men got to know each other when Bellow was at Bard in the mid-fifties, before he bought the Tivoli house.

Bellow and Chanler frequently shared dinner together, where the hard-drinking, outspoken Chanler, a "tragic or near-tragic comedian and buffoon heir of a great name," as Bellow later described him to Philip Roth, regaled Bellow with tales of his adventurous past. Chanler Chapman was the antithesis to Isaac Rosenfeld: not a trapped, yearning spirit but a free and genuinely rough one, not a Jew but a well-born WASP. Yet, as with Isaac, there was a "tragic or near-tragic" side to Chanler. His slapstick antics and loud-mouthed self-confidence seemed to Bellow to mask a troubled existential knot. As in the case of Morrie, Bellow was fascinated by but finally unable to diagnose what might lie beneath a hectoring masculine temper.

Chanler was the son of John Jay Chapman, a famous essayist, lawyer, and political reformer, author of a handbook called *Practical Agitation*, and master writer of letters. John Jay Chapman was a dyed-in-the-wool agitator. "Politics takes physique," he remarked in one letter, "and being odious takes physique. I feel like Atlas, lifting the entire universe." Chapman passed the hard-lifting trait on to his son Chanler. Both father and son had a taint of craziness to go with their strenuous practical drive. "As for insanity," commented Chapman *père*, "why, I was once examined for insanity by the two most distinguished physicians in Boston. It has no terrors. I talked to them like Plato."

The elder Chapman was suspected of insanity because he had burned off his hand in a fit of love madness. At twenty-five, while at Harvard, Chapman read Dante together with a dark-eyed fervent half-Italian girl named Minna. "The case was simple," he wrote, "but the tension was blind and terrible. I was completely unaware that I was in love." One night Chapman, strangely roiled within, sat down in front of his fireplace, tied a pair of suspenders about his left arm just above the wrist, then thrust his left hand deep into the blazing fire and held it there. When he pulled the hand out, he saw charred bones and smoking flesh. He went resolutely to Massachusetts General Hospital, was put under ether, and woke up "without the hand and very calm in my spirits," he later wrote. He now realized he was in love. It was not long before he married Minna.

Chapman's son Chanler lacked the savage masochistic impulse that the father showed when he mutilated himself. But he was, like Bellow's Henderson, volatile and rough-hewn. Once he drenched a passing couple with a pitcher of whiskey; another time he showed up at the local bank in his bathrobe to plead the case of his caretaker, who had overdrawn her account by two dollars. He walked around town in overalls, carrying a slingshot. "Who was this outrageous Ahab shaking his fist at the sea?" asked Daniel Middleton, a local journalist, about Chanler, who died in 1982.

Chanler was by turns dairy farmer, journalist, and soldier. He also wrote a book called *The Wrong Attitude: A Bad Boy at a Good School*, a memoir of his time at St. Paul's, "a great big school named after a great big powerful Saint, whom some of us boys thought a little narrow-minded." At school, in order to win a bet with a group of boys, he once filled his mouth with kerosene and struck a match in front of his face: a blaze of fire shot across the room. He sold guns to his schoolmates, too, or rather one gun, a Smith & Wesson .32, which jammed repeatedly. Chanler would buy the gun back from his dissatisfied customer and sell it to another boy.

On his Barrytown farm, Chanler used a bullhorn to command his cattle. "He seemed to know every farmer within fifty miles," notes Middleton. His stamina was legendary. Torpedoed by a U-boat during World War II, he was stranded in British Guiana and wrote to his wife, "I never had a better time in all my life." Chanler wrote a rapturous report for *Life* on his eight days in a lifeboat on the way to Guiana; there he noted, "The two things I liked best about the trip were learning to get along on very little water and sailing the lifeboat. . . . I liked nothing better than sending that swell little cockle shooting down those endless waves." Later on, Chanler served as an ambulance driver in North Africa, where he tried briefly to set up a brothel behind enemy lines.

In later years, Chanler was taunted by a cousin who asked him how he felt about the fact that his son worked as a postman, since John Jay Chapman was, according to Edmund Wilson, the greatest letter writer America had ever seen. The unruffled Chanler replied that his son was thrilled by his job, and could hardly wait for Christmas.

Bellow must have seen in Chanler an image of needy, vital activity as far removed as could be from the clenched-up Tommy Wilhelm—or his beloved Isaac Rosenfeld. If *Seize the Day* was about being trapped, *Henderson* was about being free. Like Chanler, Henderson roared, "I want! I want!" but in contrast to Isaac, he was able to put his needs into action. "Step in and enjoy the turmoil," Chanler liked to say. Chanler Chapman had a simplicity far removed from Rosenfeld's anxious nature. But Bellow was a Rosenfeld rather than a Chapman at heart, a worrier, not a man of action.

"I'm aware that it gets mixed up between comedy and earnestness," Bellow commented in a letter to the novelist Josephine Herbst in August 1959, expressing his doubts about *Henderson*. When he wrote to the writer Richard Stern that November, Bellow was more definite about the book's fault: "Every ability was brought to it except one—the talent for self-candor which so far I have been able to invest only in the *language* of what I've written. I should be able to do better than that. People are waiting. My own soul is waiting." With *Herzog* the wait would be over.

CHAPTER 4

Sondra Tschacbasov and Jack Ludwig

When he wrote *Herzog*, Bellow hit a nerve. The book reached the best seller list in October 1964, and quickly ascended to the top; it stayed at number one for a little over six months, until mid-May 1965. *Herzog* was not manically profane like Roth's *Portnoy's Complaint*, which stuck its richly obscene tongue out at America and its Jews five years later, causing a scandalous *shonde*-quake heard round the Jewish world, but it was just as intent on unsettling readers in what would come to seem a distinctively Jewish way, by bringing an agitated psyche out into the open.

Herzog was in many ways an improbable candidate for bestsellerdom. Here was a novel about a failed professor, a nervous wreck who spent his time writing letters to famous men living and dead, when he wasn't meditating revenge on his estranged wife and her lover. The book was peppered with references to philosophers and religious thinkers: Buber, Berdyaev, Heidegger. It was an overwrought book, soaked in anxiety, full of what Jews call *tsures*. In *Herzog* Bellow made the emotionally muddled Jewish intellectual a novelistic hero. He joined obsessive rumination with comedy and sensuality: his novel was for long stretches a thought-monologue, but at the same time awash in perverse, colorful human presences. The book is transparently autobiographical, a slumming tour of the author's tragical farce of a marriage. No one, John Berryman wrote to Bellow, had so far "wallow[ed] with full art" the way he had done in *Herzog*.

What accounts for *Herzog*'s appeal to a public otherwise devoted to taut suspense tales like John le Carré's *The Spy Who Came in from the Cold* or topical potboilers like Bel Kaufman's *Up the Down Staircase*, about a teacher at an inner-city school, and Irving Wallace's *The Man*, about the first black president, all of them best sellers in 1964? The answer lies in the way Bellow tied his culture's crisis to the trauma of an individual soul, a man separated from his children, betrayed by his wife, the strident, wrathful Madeleine, and his best friend, ruddy, wooden-legged Valentine Gersbach. The well-worn themes of the era flow through Herzog: alienation, anomie, the organization man. Bellow's hero strikes out against the "lousy, cringing, grudging conception of human nature" that was "Protestant Freudianism" in the early sixties, the golden age of psychoanalysis in America. Herzog, who writes letters to presidents and generals as well as philosophers, bears witness to the enthrallment of intellectuals with political power during the Kennedy years. The love affair is absurdly one-sided. No one writes back to Herzog: he never even mails his letters.

Bellow once gave a capsule summary of *Herzog* that went something like this: A man's wife ditches him, and he turns to Spinoza. There is something unstoppably comical about Herzog's flurry of letters to Herr Nietzsche, Doktor Professor Heidegger, and the others. The big minds won't help him out of his emotional morass. Yet Bellow never plays philosophy for laughs. In *Herzog* he takes up in an utterly different key Henry James's question about the meeting between European ways of thinking and American life, a question that the American novelists between James and Bellow had for the most part ignored. And even for James Europe was not an intellectual presence so much as a rigorous source of social distinctions and habits. Bellow's Herzog is strung between life and high ideas and approaches both in full, desperate earnest. He is in this respect a rarity among the heroes of the American novel.

What most interests Bellow in *Herzog* is the troubled heart. His own trouble is front and center in the book: the affair between his second wife, Sondra Tschacbasov, and his close friend Jack Ludwig. In Bellow's novel, the crass and hearty Ludwig, who had a clubfoot, becomes the unforgettable peg-legged Gersbach. This crude showman-shaman worshipfully attaches himself to Herzog just as Ludwig did to Bellow. From time to time, when he's not flattering Herzog, Gersbach lets loose short bursts of scorn at the man he has cuckolded.

The other troubles that Bellow's novel evokes reach far beyond the ruin of his marriage. *Herzog* is, in the Jewish sense of the word, a prophetic book. Hosea, too, was done wrong by a bad woman: so Madeleine's departure unleashes high thoughts in Herzog. Like Job, he refuses to accept suffering as reasonable. Restless, he demands answers. Herzog's sorrows are not just personal; they ask for an unreachable justice. Full of pain, he visits a city courtroom and sees a pair of defendants who have murdered a small boy, "Lying down to copulate, and standing up to kill." Bellow will revisit this same wounded theme, the disordered, violent life, two decades later in *The Dean's December.* In *Herzog* the glimpse of ravaged murderous poverty is almost too much for Moses, and for us, to bear; it brings out our unsettled, futile wish to heal the world. The radical impulse at the heart of the courtroom scene—its *Herz*—is sorrow for the sheer wrongness of the state of things. Herzog has some kinship with Malamud's talented sufferers, although Bellow, unlike Malamud, never turns Herzog's pain into a shrewd, stifling ascetic vocation. His suffering is more open, a public question.

American intellectuals of the fifties and early sixties were often complacent judges who chided the culture for its shortcomings: its lack of deep thought, its materialism. But Herzog is no such calm master. He is consciously vain, buffeted by his passions, and rancorous, not least against Madeleine, who looks to Herzog like an iron-willed, self-adoring fiend. Herzog, like Hamlet, rips into "woman," when he's not enjoying the homely comforts his girlfriends give him.

Herzog wins no prizes for male sensitivity to woman's plight: Bellow is honest on this score, perhaps to a fault.

Bellow's earliest conflict appeared in *Augie March*: the literary soul's battle with the brass-tacks business world that his father and brothers represented. Next in Bellow's career came the breaking down of intellectual defenses, his tour of Reichian therapy, the weeping Tommy Wilhelm and the wild man Henderson. *Herzog* carries further Bellow's doubts about lofty mental posturing. By the late fifties Bellow had become skeptical about the New York intellectual way of looking down on America from above. Herzog crumbles to pieces, defeated by ex-wives, leaky pipes, and indecision; he knows that high-mindedness won't save him. And so he becomes a romantic and returns to the sources of feeling, the early family life that he remembers from Jewish immigrant Montreal and Chicago.

Herzog recalls his "ancient times," "remoter than Egypt," life as a child on Napoleon Street in Montreal; his father with his smoker's cough, his mother who "did the wash, and mourned," his brother Shura (Morrie), who "with staring disingenuous eyes was plotting to master the world," his brother Willie's (Sam's) asthma—"Trying to breathe he gripped the table and rose on his toes like a cock about to crow"— and finally "his soft prim sister who played the piano": Jane, the eldest Bellow sibling.

These are some of the novel's best pages, with a heartfelt paean to Jewish memory: "The children of the race, by a never-failing miracle, opened their eyes on one strange world after another, age after age, and uttered the same prayer in each, eagerly loving what they found. What was wrong with Napoleon Street? thought Herzog. All he ever wanted was there." But it's not true. Herzog wants more: a chapter after his memory of Napoleon Street, Moses the Jew rests in uneasy erotic bliss with his girlfriend Ramona while an Egyptian singer croons "Mi Port Said." Finally *Herzog* centers not on childhood reminiscence but on the trials of grown-up sexuality. And at the core of those trials is Madeleine, who was originally Sondra.

———

SONDRA TSCHACBASOV met Bellow in 1952, when she was twenty-one. After Bennington, Philip Rahv had hired her to be a receptionist at *Partisan Review* even though she couldn't type, couldn't take dictation, and was a bad speller. She had exotic flair, though. Sondra, also known as Sasha, mesmerized men: to parties she would wear a low-cut black dress with a heavy silver Maltese cross between her breasts, hair piled high on her head. One day Bellow called the *Partisan Review* office and Sondra answered. You must be the new girl, he said. It wasn't long before Bellow started dating Sondra, who was living in the Ansonia Hotel on the Upper West Side, later the setting of *Seize the Day*.

Bellow was teaching at Princeton at the time, and he took Sondra to a wild party there. A drunken Berryman recited his poetry flat on his back while caressing Sondra's foot. Years later Sondra remembered that R. W. B. Lewis, her teacher at Bennington, asked "point-blank if I was sleeping with Saul yet, because they were all placing bets."

Sondra's insouciant posturing put off the women at the party, and they despised her wild attractiveness to the *PR* circle's men. But her seeming poise came from insecurity: at twenty-one, she was out of her depth in this intellectual and emotional shark tank.

We know much more than we did before about Sondra Tschacbasov thanks to Zachary Leader's Bellow biography. Leader relies on an unpublished memoir by Sondra which reveals that her father, a modernist painter friendly with Adolph Gottlieb and Mark Rothko, sexually abused her from the time she was twelve through high school, when the family lived in the Chelsea Hotel. This long-running trauma left a heavy mark on Sondra. *Herzog* alludes to the abuse in veiled terms, and relays as well Bellow's suspicion that she might have been inventing it—Sondra was known to fictionalize her past, claiming, for example, that her family were emigrés who had fled the Russian Revolution. In part as a result of her father's abuse, Sondra was hungry for authority. The handsome, charismatic Bishop Fulton Sheen converted Sondra to Catholicism in December 1952: he called her his *dushka* ("the Russian word for soul," he said).

Sondra was attracted to Bellow as a sober, work-minded man with a strict writing routine. "What a relief from my whirling dervish of a parent, all untrammeled passions and unbridled habits and desires," she wrote in her memoir. But Bellow's professional anxiety and his rigid character soon led to trouble. Early in their marriage there were heated arguments about money (he thought she was extravagant), about sex ("you expect too much," Bellow charged), about her neglect of housework. Bellow briefly persuaded her to see a Reichian therapist. Stuck in the vast, ramshackle Tivoli house, Sondra became an upstate Emma Bovary desperate for romantic escape.

Escape came in the unlikely form of Bellow's colleague Jack Ludwig. Bellow and Ludwig first met at a party given by Chanler Chapman for new Bard faculty in 1953. Leader reports that Keith Botsford, who taught at Bard, remembered Ludwig as a backwoods Canadian Jew with a loud, low voice: "A bulky Winnipeg hockey body, a heft arm leaning against the wall, a mass of hair, bristling and thick." Ludwig accosted Bellow with back-slapping laughter and what Bellow called "butcher boy Yiddish," and Botsford had to rescue him from the over-hearty Ludwig's clutches.

When Sondra first met Ludwig at a party later that same year, just before the Bard term started, she was feeling alienated from the faculty wives and cocktail-sipping husbands. Suddenly, she remembered, "this very round faced, fat guy, wearing a hideous checked jacket that even a bookie might have rejected, gave me a joyful, humorous smile." And they were off—though it would be five years before the affair between Sondra and Jack began.

Sondra wrote in her memoir that Ludwig and Bellow were two starkly different personalities. "Ludwig was very expansive, warm, big, big-hearted, . . . a larger than life character." But Saul looked at the world askance—"His head was always [slightly] turned away from you, . . . like a magpie, going to take something and use it."

The affair between Sondra and Jack began in Tivoli in

May or June 1958. Since the birth of Adam in January 1957, the Sondra-Saul relationship had been more fractured than ever. Sondra was relying on both Jack and his wife, Leya, for emotional support against Bellow. "Saul was disapproving, constantly finding fault, selfish beyond belief in every way in bed and out," Sondra recalled. At the same time Bellow was seeking out Jack's marital advice, complaining (in Sondra's later words) that "I was too demanding, imperious, too centered around the baby, immature, spoiled, a sexual flop." While Leya was in labor with their second child, and Jack and Sondra sat in the hospital waiting room, Jack revealed to Sondra Saul's complaints about her. He also told her about Bellow's infidelities, which, he said, were common knowledge at Bard. Jack had been coming to the Tivoli house to talk to Sondra over coffee in the late mornings, while Bellow was still working. He became her brotherly confidant, then one day he confessed—don't you know? he asked—that he loved her. Soon after, their affair began.

Meanwhile, Ludwig had attached himself even more firmly to Bellow than to Sondra. On walks Ludwig would join Bellow in Reichian roaring, then give him sex advice. He imitated Bellow's expressions and mannerisms, his way of talking. "He wanted to *be* Saul Bellow," remarked a student who knew them both.

Bellow was offered a job teaching at the University of Minnesota for the fall of 1958. He accepted on one condition: that Ludwig also be given a position. He was, and the Bellows and Ludwigs moved to Minneapolis. That fall Sondra decided to end the affair, but she wavered, and soon she was sleeping with both Bellow and Ludwig. In the spring of 1959 she had an abortion, unknown to Bellow. That summer, back in Tivoli, she knew she had to get out. In October, in Minneapolis, she announced to Bellow that their marriage was over.

Sondra only gradually became the vengeful, driven fury who tormented Moses Herzog. In the early days of their relationship, Bellow thought he was the master and teacher, with Sondra his eager pupil. In a letter to Berryman probably written sometime in 1954, near the beginning of his romance with Sondra, Bellow wrote, "A young girl requires making. A man makes her into a woman. Whither then? I hope she'll become my wife, but it is a great thing to have waked someone into life, and Sasha is a very considerable human being." Sleeping Beauty was Bellow's favorite fairy tale: he must have seen himself as the fortunate prince who had not only woken Sondra up, but also shaped her, Pygmalion style. In the end, though, his creation had a mind of her own. When Jack declared his love for her, Sondra wrote in her memoir, "I looked into his eyes, really looked, and somehow fell into them. A coup de foudre. . . . I was Sleeping Beauty." Now Jack was her awakener, her prince. By the time Sondra walked out, in October 1959, Bellow had revised his story line of their relationship. The next month, he wrote to Keith Botsford, "Sasha is an absolutist. I think I've loved even *that*, in her. I believe I learned with her how to love a woman." He had come to adore Sondra's dominating will, her effort to take control over her wounded psyche.

All along Sondra proved decisive, determined, not least

in her work habits. She was an obsessive student. In October 1958 Bellow wrote to his editor Pat Covici that his wife was reading medieval history "sixteen hours a day and has little time for anything else," and in a letter to Ellison he said, "Boring subjects delight her." Bellow had met someone who outdid even him in her work ethic: Sondra, so much younger than her husband, was declaring herself his superior.

In January 1959 Bellow wrote to Josie Herbst about the "blowup" between him and Sondra the preceding June. "She took the kid and went to the city," Bellow lamented. "I had to hold together the house and my impossible book and take care of my older son who came to spend the summer with me." During this time Bellow was revising *Henderson*, dictating to a typist "eight, ten, twelve and fourteen hours a day for six weeks." After the rocky summer of 1958, Bellow said to Herbst, he and Sondra had "patched things up" back in Minneapolis. She had been suffering from a nervous disorder, he was convinced. In February 1959 Bellow reported to Covici that "Sondra too is much better. All's well in the sack, unusually well, and we've begun to feel much affection for each other." Bellow's word "begun," like his choice of "affection" rather than "love," looks ominous—Bellow and Sondra had been together for four years at this point. Before the year was out, their marriage would be history.

HERZOG's opening line rings with a desperate man's strange wit: "If I am out of my mind, it's all right with me, thought Moses Herzog." Madeleine, Moses' wife, has walked out on him, and so he spends his time writing letters to the famous dead, to public figures, and to his own dead friends. Herzog sits alone in his house in the Berkshires, surrounded by the shards of his scholarly work on romanticism. While he was gone, hikers camped out in the house and left a used tampon on his desk. Here in the backwoods non-town of Ludeyville, too small to be found on any map, Herzog eats beans from the can with white bread. A rat, he notices, has tunneled through the loaf.

Not much happens in *Herzog*. Moses, shaking himself into action, buys some summer clothes. He decides to take a vacation on Martha's Vineyard, then changes his mind. He remembers his affairs with a Polish woman, Wanda, and a Japanese woman, Sono, and he thinks often of his current girlfriend, Ramona. He remembers, with sharp pain, his discovery of the affair between Madeleine and Gersbach. On a trip back to Chicago to see his and Madeleine's little daughter, Junie, Herzog takes along his dead father's pistol and some of his Russian rubles. He is thinking of shooting Gersbach: a silly idea, he knows. Like Dmitri Karamazov, he will kill no one. Instead he has a small traffic accident with Junie in the car, the police discover the pistol and the rubles, and he is briefly arrested. The book ends with Herzog back in Ludeyville, getting ready for an evening date with Ramona, who is coming to visit him.

Bellow takes aim at himself more directly in *Herzog* than ever before or since in his fiction. The hero knows full well how ludicrous, how vengeful, he can be. Some readers think Bellow was moved by self-pity more than anything else when he wrote *Herzog*. But soon after the novel begins Herzog rapidly, flatly indicts himself, admitting "that he had been a bad husband—twice," "a loving but bad father," and "an ungrateful child."

Herzog is a far more actual father than Henderson or Tommy Wilhelm. He knows the pain that comes with missing his children. And *Herzog*'s picture of a child with her father is the most tender of all its tableaux. Herzog remembers his little daughter Junie, who here stands in for Adam: "She stood on her father's lap to comb his hair. His thighs were trodden by her feet. He embraced her small bones with fatherly hunger while her breath on his face stirred his deepest feelings." To be separated from one's children is a cruel fate, and Bellow knew this fate well. "I sometimes long for Adam," he wrote to the lawyer Jonas Schwartz in October 1960, begging that Sondra send "one postcard a month" about the boy.

Bellow's portrait of Madeleine is cold and raging, just like Mady herself. Adam Bellow, who is Sondra's son as well as Saul's, told me, "It was impossible to recognize my mother in that portrait. I told him when I was fifteen," Adam added, speaking calmly, "that woman is not my mother." Herzog sees in Mady only a relentless blind narcissism. Herzog too has his narcissism, but unlike Mady, he senses his foolish side, whereas she takes herself with utter, steely earnest. It was Sondra's icy composure that most perturbed Bellow and convinced him that her heart was cold and alien too. Bellow wrote to Pat Covici in November 1959, when he was still in the dark about Sondra and Jack, "I have good grounds, many, many wounds to hate her for. But I'm not very good at it, and I succeed best when I think of her as her father's daughter. For she is Tschacbasov. She has a Tschacbasov heart—an insect heart." Bellow's use of "insect" comes from *The Brothers Karamazov*, where it means perverse, greedy, and plotting. Bellow wrote to the novelist Stanley Elkin in 1992 that "old Tschacbasov . . . was a repulsive old phony and low self-dramatizer, a would-be Father Karamazov but without intelligence or wit."

Bellow thought Sondra had inherited her father's insect-like cold mastery, though he knew his young wife was also shaken by self-doubt. She was at her most chilly and decisive when she finally told Bellow she wanted a divorce. "Anyway she walked into the living room with icy control about three weeks ago and told me she wanted a divorce," Bellow wrote in his letter to Covici. "There's no one else involved. There doesn't need to be. She does everything on principle, a perfect ideologist." And so it happens in *Herzog*. When Mady rejects Moses, she touches narcissistic triumph: "Her color grew very rich, and her brows, and that Byzantine nose of hers, rose, moved; her blue eyes gained by the flush that kept deepening, rising from her chest and her throat. She was in an ecstasy of consciousness."

Mady loves to admire herself in the mirror, gazing at "the great blue eyes, the vivid bangs, the medallion profile. The satisfaction she took in herself was positively plural—imperial," Moses remembers. A Jewish convert like Sondra, Mady clings to her Catholicism as a bulwark against her crazy upbringing. Her parents were bohemians: her mother fragile, her father a vain theatrical impresario—"You know how I learned my ABC's? From Lenin's *State and Revolution*. Those people are insane!" weeps Mady.

Herzog is full of snapshots of fury: Bellow shows Mady utterly out of control, absorbed in the richness of her rage. In the country, on the rocks with Mady, Herzog plays his oboe while she storms off in the car. (Bellow was an accomplished recorder player who loved to perform at parties.) Pregnant Mady shrieks as she denounces her husband, who notes the "wild blue glare" of her eyes, her nostrils trembling with indignation. She seems not a woman but an unnatural force.

Like Mady, Gersbach, a near-mythic beast, rides the chariot of narcissism in *Herzog*. Gersbach, Herzog muses, resembles Hitler's pianist Putzi Hanfstaengel—a palpable hit. "But Gersbach had a pair of extraordinary eyes for a red-haired man, brown, deep, hot eyes, full of life. The lashes, too, were vital, ruddy-dark, long and childlike. And that hair was bearishly thick." Gersbach, like Jack Ludwig, speaks a mangled kitchen-table Yiddish full of errors. (Bellow's friend Stuart Brent, according to his son Jonathan, loved to talk Yiddish with Bellow until Bellow, pained by Brent's mistakes, ordered him to speak English.) After he corrects Gersbach's Yiddish during a winter walk in Minnesota, with "Gersbach in his great storm coat, belted, bareheaded, exhaling vapor, kicking through the snow with the all-battering leg," Herzog thinks, "Dealing with Valentine was like dealing with a king. He had a thick grip. He might have held a scepter. He was a king, an emotional king, and the depth of his heart was his kingdom."

"But Gersbach almost always cried, and it was strange," Moses ruminates. He concedes that Gersbach has suffered more than he has, during "his agony under the wheels of the boxcar" when, as a boy, he lost his leg. "Gersbach's tormented face was stony white, pierced by the radiant bristles of his red beard. His lower lip had almost disappeared beneath the upper. His great, his hot sorrow! Molten sorrow!" Gersbach's performing ardor *is* his reality: he leans on it like a wooden leg.

Gersbach is the life of the party, a romping knave who far outstrips Moses' sad involuntary clowning. He is, Herzog comes to realize, a heroic fraud: "Innocent. Sadistic. Dancing around. Instinctive. Heartless. . . . Laughing at jokes. Deep, too. Exclaiming 'I *love* you!' or 'This I *believe*.' And while moved by these 'beliefs' he steals you blind." Gersbach is the opposite of Herzog, focused and certain, with total belief in himself. His pride naturally appeals to Mady.

Looking for escape from his thoughts of narcissistic Mady and rapacious Gersbach, Herzog seeks out the cultured seductress Ramona, a flower-shop owner of exotic mixed ancestry. Ramona captivates Moses with her continental flair. "She walked with quick efficiency," Bellow says of Ramona, "rapping her heels in energetic Castilian style. . . . She entered a room provocatively, swaggering slightly, one hand touching her thigh, as though she carried a knife in her garter belt." The Japanese Sono is an even more exotic girlfriend, given a tender portrait by Bellow. Like

Ramona, Sono is a latter-day Calypso, adept at pampering her man. The comforts these two women offer—the beautiful dinners, hot baths, massages—are the weary traveler's delight; they give the flavor of home without the strife of marriage. With both Ramona and Sono, Moses becomes a grateful boy, while the woman is maternal giver, playmate, and pal. The fragile, even foolish character of such idylls doesn't keep Bellow from treasuring them, in *Herzog* as in the later *Humboldt's Gift*.

The real-life basis for Ramona, Rosette Lamont, was an Ionesco scholar, a professor of literature in New York, and a glamorous, brilliant figure in Bellow's life. In 1974 she wrote a reminiscence of Bellow's years in Tivoli for the magazine *Mosaic*. Lamont's essay shows that she adores Bellow. "The profile is that of a witty, half-domesticated fox," she writes. "Cheeks, mouth and chin are soft, the vulnerable clay of a thinker. Exquisitely delicate, high-arched feet suggest the aristocrat, the dandy." But there are some hilarious bursts of tongue in cheek too. She describes Bellow answering his correspondence. "The most arduous task," Lamont says, "was that of dealing with the trail of women left throughout European capitals." Lamont adds that "Bellow rarely gets involved with the so-called liberated female, and if it happens by accident, the results are disastrous."

Rosette Lamont lost out to Susan Glassman in the marriage race: it was Susan, not Rosette, who became Bellow's third wife. But in fiction Rosette won. Ramona and Herzog end the novel together, as Moses prepares on *Herzog*'s last page to welcome her to Ludeyville. The upbeat ending of *Herzog* drew mixed reactions when the book was published: if this was a tale of midlife breakdown, some critics complained, it should come to a more dire end. Lamont herself reviewed *Herzog* for the *Massachusetts Review*, and she praised the "wonderful sense of peace" at the novel's end.

In her essay-memoir Lamont depicts Bellow's fine unregulated manhood surrounded by pickers and stealers, especially women. Bellow to her mind is a noble and dashing knight but one under great duress. In *Herzog* Moses feels the urge to escape, and so did Bellow. At one point during a heated parley with the lawyer Sandor Himmelstein about his marital woes, Moses hears a ship's horn out on Lake Michigan. "Herzog would have given anything to be a deckhand bound for Duluth," Bellow writes.

Bellow was living through a crack-up in late 1959, after Sondra walked out. Early the following year he wrote to the Viking editor Marshall Best, "If I hadn't gone off in November [to Europe] I might now be in the loony bin and not in London. This has a metaphorical sound but I mean it literally." Bellow was in Europe until March 1960, in part on a lecture tour sponsored by the State Department. His divorce from Sondra became final in June.

Moses' saving grace is his lack of resolution. *Herzog*'s odd, thwarted climax occurs when with his father's antique gun in his hand, he sees "Uncle Val" giving Junie a bath. Here Gersbach is Quilty to Herzog's Humbert, as Moses reflects, "To shoot him—an absurd thought! As soon as Herzog saw the actual person giving an actual bath, the reality of it, the tenderness of such a buffoon to a little child, his intended violence turned into *theater*, into something ludicrous." Herzog never seriously contemplates murder. (Nor did Bellow, though he seems to have suggested to friends that he might shoot Ludwig.) Instead, he is touched by the tender gesture of his clownish enemy.

Bellow finally discovered Sondra's affair in the fall of 1960, after the divorce was final. Months later, in early 1961, he wrote a letter to Ludwig that remains a small masterpiece of acerbic wit. Soon after, the agonized Bellow jumped into writing a novel about his wrecked marriage: *Herzog* was the four-hundred-page extension of the letter.

In his letter, Bellow admitted to Ludwig that

> I haven't got the sharpest eyes in the world; I'm not superman but superidiot. Only a giant among idiots would marry Sondra and offer you friendship. God knows I am not stainless faultless Bellow. I leave infinities on every side to be desired. But love her as my wife? Love you as a friend? I might as well have gone to work for Ringling Brothers and been shot out of the cannon twice a day. At least they would have let me wear a costume.

The Saul, Sondra, and Jack triangle that produced the wonder of *Herzog* was a three-ring circus. Astonishingly, there was more to come. The vexed relation between real people and the fictional characters based on them has rarely taken on so bizarre and fascinating a form.

Ludwig's three-year job at Minnesota was ending. He

was a popular teacher, and well-known to the public too: he taught a class on educational television called "Humanities in the Modern World." Three hundred students signed a petition begging the administration to keep Ludwig, and his colleagues pleaded his case too, to no avail. But Ludwig landed on his feet: he secured a job at SUNY Stony Brook and got tenure there. Jack and Sondra continued their affair after the move to Long Island.

Meanwhile, the roman à clef tangle became stranger still. In an act of high-wire chutzpah, Ludwig reviewed *Herzog* favorably for *Holiday* magazine, pausing only to deride Herzog's (that is, Bellow's) "siege of self-justification." Ludwig punctured Herzog's claims to victimhood and also denounced his "tasteless" remarks about "'cripples.'" At the end of his review, Ludwig named Bellow, along with Ralph Ellison, the heir to Hemingway and Faulkner. He proclaimed that "the novel is in good hands. *Herzog* is here to stay." Years later, Bellow wrote to Kazin that Ludwig's review of *Herzog* was "ingenious, shrewd, supersubtle, shamanistic, Rasputin-like." Ludwig also lectured on Bellow at the Modern Language Association, to an audience of nearly a thousand people drawn by the hope of scandalous tidbits.

Finally, and most outrageously, Ludwig's next novel, *Above Ground*, was a dreadfully written revision of *Herzog*, this time told from the seducer's rather than the husband's point of view. The Bellow figure, Louie, is a sculptor rather than a writer, but his real identity is clear. The Ludwig character suffers constantly because he is unable to choose between his wife and his mistress. By the time *Above Ground* was published, in 1966, Jack and Sondra's relationship had fallen apart, giving Ludwig a free hand to come down on Sondra even harder than Bellow had.

Ludwig's *Above Ground* apes *Herzog* in style and subject matter, with some intermissions for inept Joycean stream of consciousness. It is a dismal, nearly unreadable slog except for one incendiary section near the end, a series of letters from Mavra, the Sondra character: a part of the book so much better than the rest it might have been written by someone else. And perhaps—so some have speculated—it was. "The letters of the heroine are conspicuously superior in style, but the book is garbage," Bellow wrote suspiciously to Sondra.

Mavra's letters are wicked, pornographic, and taunting. She tells Josh (Ludwig) about her casual pick-ups, her insatiable sexual curiosity: "I threw one leg up on the couch and he just had to stroke upwards. . . . I mean I can get something started and like a spectator watch it unfold—like a movie I've never seen." She blends grandiose erotic fantasy with low-down vengefulness. She tells Josh, "We can do terrible things to each other, let strangers into our beds, but on the highest level be priest and priestess, shuck off dead snakeskin and be born again, younger, more beautiful. Please don't tell me—or think—this is rationale."

In another letter Mavra waxes resentful, threatening, insecure:

> I could maybe stand you taking a bitch to bed. But if you loved her I'd slit my throat. . . . I want a

> detailed checklist, to bury the past and establish my primacy (sp?).
>
> You'd say sure Titsy was great and Snatchy was terrific and Dimple-ass was lovely but Mavra Mavra you are the greatest. . . . I'd say how great was Titsy, really, and you'd say Titsy had a frozen pelvis and screwed as if she was in a dentist's chair, was middlebrow, smelled all wrong, had hair like a Barbie Doll's, was always dry, peed like a horse, put on a big show but never came once in her life, not even at her own hand. We'd bury them all like that, one after the other, and never send flowers.

The verbal tics are Sondra's: she was unsure of her spelling. And some of the jokes must have been hers, too ("If I had like Rebecca to carry an urn of water I'd slosh it all over the intermediaries," she tells Josh). Ludwig, it seems, wanted Bellow to think that these were Sondra's true confessions, that he had copied them from her hand.

Ludwig takes Bellow's side against Sondra in *Above Ground*. He even makes Mavra condemn herself. Louie is a fool and a "playactor," Mavra says, but she herself is the guilty one: she mauled his psyche for the sheer pleasure of it. "That was really *me*, dirty *me*. Turning love into a murderous *anti* thing, to cut a sad man like Louie to bits." Maggie, Josh's wife, says to him, "She engineered the fights with Louie, the flight to the city; the whole scenario worked out as she wrote it. . . . She can manipulate settings, environments. Like a middling fighter, Josh, she picks her spots."

For Ludwig, Sondra, with her insect soul, was the sadistic author of the whole disastrous romantic triangle.

"The tragedies of my life were not over Saul. They were over Ludwig," Sondra wrote many years later in her memoir. Later still, Ludwig revealed his final word on the matter in an email to Bellow's biographer Zachary Leader: "Saul was hurt. By his friend. That's it."

HERZOG MADE BELLOW a famous and wealthy man. The late sixties were years of celebrity for him, but much of the money he made would go to alimony and child support, especially after his ill-fated third marriage to Susan Glassman. In 1961, the same year he moved back to Chicago to teach at the university, and about a year and a half after his divorce from Sondra, Bellow married Susan, an ex-girlfriend of Philip Roth. Their marriage lasted a scant five years, until 1966. Its rancorous aftermath stretched over an additional decade, as Susan pursued Bellow through the courts, trying to secure a larger share of his income.

Bellow had first met Susan in 1957. He was giving a talk at the University of Chicago Hillel, and the young Roth attended with Susan. After Bellow's lecture, Susan went up to chat with him. She would soon switch her allegiance from Roth to Bellow. When Bellow's marriage to Sondra broke up, Susan was there waiting.

Susan, the daughter of a prominent Chicago surgeon, became Bellow's intellectual confidante as well as his lover. She encouraged him through his feverish, excited work on

Herzog, some of it done while Bellow, then chronically short of money, was teaching at the University of Puerto Rico for a few months at the beginning of 1961. Keith Botsford, his old Bard colleague who was also teaching at Puerto Rico, got Bellow the job. In San Juan Botsford proved himself a dedicated friend and an eccentric whirlwind of energy, but the tropical heat, Bellow wrote, always gave him "the depressed sense of having come out of the movies at midday." Bellow's letters to Susan from Puerto Rico are energetic, erotic, breathlessly high-pitched. "From your nutty but devoted and adoring lover," he wrote, "here are a few pages more of this impossible *Herzog* whom I love like a foster brother."

Bellow's marriage to Susan was on the rocks almost as soon as it started. While Bellow typed manically, Susan devoted herself to decorating the couple's lavish new Chicago apartment. She loved socializing and tennis, and delighted in being the wife of a famous novelist. Bellow, with his strict work ethic—five hours a day at his desk, then the afternoon reserved either for teaching or cruising through the streets of Chicago with old friends, his main method of novelistic research—was often at odds with Susan. His new wife was a voracious and alert reader who wrote short stories that she hoped to publish. She was a more than fit intellectual companion for Bellow, but, just like Sondra, she disdained Bellow's friendships with the Chicago pals of his youth, and criticized his Montreal relatives as crude Yiddish-speaking proletarians.

Bellow's strenuous writing routine continued after his

third marriage fell apart. Adam, Bellow's son from his marriage to Sondra, was three when his parents were divorced. During his childhood he lived alternately with his father and mother, and spent much time in the apartment on East Fifty-Fifth Street in Chicago's Hyde Park that Bellow shared with Susan and later lived in alone, after Susan's departure. "He used to work up a sweat," Adam told me. "He would stink up the house, literally, because he'd start working in the morning without taking a shower. He'd be sitting there in his bathrobe, with the sun coming in across Lake Michigan." Thomas Mann's children remembered their father's perpetually closed study door. Bellow's son recalls him not closeted off but in the middle of things, furiously writing, with the phone ringing and domestic life bouncing on around him.

It was Bellow's affair with Maggie Staats, whom he met in early 1966, that endangered his marriage to Susan. Maggie, who was then twenty-four—twenty-seven years younger than Bellow—was a typist at *The New Yorker* who had studied literature at Northwestern and Yale; she later became a magazine editor. She was from an old East Coast family, and was not only sharply intelligent but blonde, pert-nosed, and pixielike. It wasn't long before Bellow was talking marriage to her, but she rebuffed him. Maggie Staats (later Simmons) was married five times, and through it all remained close friends with Bellow.

Maggie's relationship with Bellow was on-and-off, but it was always intimate and electric. Maggie later summed up her years with Bellow with one word: wonderful. "I miss you so much, it's like sickness, or hunger," Bellow wrote to Maggie near the beginning of their affair, "childish love-sickness." There were other women too, among them the exuberant painter Arlette Landes. Both Maggie and Arlette would be depicted in *Humboldt's Gift*: Maggie with great tenderness, Arlette less so.

Bellow connected his headlong love for Maggie Staats to his ardent belief in the importance of childhood memories. In a journal passage from mid-1966, the fifty-one-year-old Bellow wrote,

> Unwillingness, reluctance to recognize the reality of the present moment because of attachment to something in childhood.
>
> Therefore a brother rather than a father to the children. . . .
>
> Locate the Old System with passion—not so other things.
>
> Maggie is part of this. Has the purity of earliest connections. Miraculous to have accomplished so much in the world while in such bondage.

The Old System was Bellow's term for the tangled bank of early family relationships, always the most intense locale for him. In 1966 he was working on his story with that title, about a man who pays his estranged sister twenty thousand dollars so that he can see her on her deathbed. Parts of the story were borrowed from Bellow's Montreal relatives, the Gameroffs, but it spoke to Bellow's own sweet, pained knowledge that his earliest attachments had formed him indelibly, that there was no substitute for the first love of mother, father, and siblings. "He kept making and breaking families, but his only real family was the original family," Adam Bellow remarked to me. "He just loved them all. That's how he apprehended people, through the innocent power of love." Because Maggie Staats shared in the "purity of earliest connections" that is both nostalgic freedom and "bondage," as Bellow put it in his journal, she was, to his mind, his truest companion.

Bellow's separation from Susan came in 1966; they were divorced two years later. He now had three sons by three different wives (and, he once joked, by "three different husbands"). Stretched thin by the money he owed, and aching from the ruin of yet another marriage, Bellow looked to his constant anchor, novel writing. "He wanted to be a patriarch," Adam Bellow remembered, "but he wasn't very good at it. He wasn't very easy in his conscience, and he didn't like having us [his sons] together." While his marriage to Susan broke apart, Bellow started writing a novel about a man of solid conscience, a man profoundly unlike both Herzog and Herzog's creator: Artur Sammler.

CHAPTER 5

Edward Shils

MORE THAN THREE DECADES after *Herzog*, Bellow confessed in a letter to Philip Roth that when he wrote the book he had been too close to his title character. As a result, Bellow said, Herzog was a "chump" and a "sentimentalist." Even in the first wake of *Herzog*'s vast success, Bellow must have felt the urge toward a different kind of hero, someone more assured and Olympian, superior to the unstable Herzog with his restless heart. The now middle-aged novelist invented in his next book a hero who could claim a moral advantage that Herzog had lacked. He produced the Artur Sammler of *Mr. Sammler's Planet*, a "Polish-Oxonian" Jew transplanted from the doomed Europe of the thirties and forties to crazy late sixties New York.

Bellow modeled Sammler's character, at least in part, on the man who had gotten him his job at the University of Chicago's Committee on Social Thought, the haughty, formality-bound sociologist Edward Shils. Renowned in his field, Shils was from a working-class Jewish background, but he put on a rather stiff, donnish air; he used a walking stick and annotated papers and manuscripts scrupulously in his characteristic green ink. Shils spoke with a hauteur like Dr. Johnson's, wore nothing but tweeds, and cultivated an intellectual superiority that frightened off many students and colleagues, though he could be a generous, affectionate teacher too—at least outside of class.

"I love Edward," Bellow said early on in his friendship with Shils. For most of the sixties, the two men were inseparable. But their close bond would not survive long after *Mr. Sammler's Planet* came out in 1970. Shortly after *Sammler* was published, Shils and Bellow began to quarrel. Shils, in his green ink, had abundantly annotated the rough draft of *Sammler.* But now Bellow began to irritate Shils. What rankled most of all was Bellow's effort to promote the careers of two of his girlfriends, Edith Hartnett and Bette Howland, at the prestigious Committee on Social Thought. He tried to secure tenure for Hartnett, an accomplished scholar, but Shils stood in the door. "I refuse to let him use the Committee as a rest home for his old *nafkes*" (whores, in Yiddish), muttered Shils. Bellow retaliated in kind: in one letter, he called Shils an "unlanced boil." The friendship had fallen apart. When Bellow tried to mend fences years later by visiting Shils on his deathbed, Shils refused to see him, announcing, "I have no wish to ease the conscience of that son of a bitch."

In *Humboldt's Gift* Shils appears as Professor Richard Durnwald, an honest, brave devotee of the life of the mind and a superior conversationalist. Though his relationship with Shils had soured by the time *Humboldt* was published in 1975, Bellow's brief portrait of him in that novel lacks any satirical twists. Those would come later, in *Ravelstein*.

ARTUR SAMMLER IS the only elevated, refined superego figure in Bellow's novels. But he is not perfectly armored: far from it. Sammler's name means "collector" in German and Yiddish. He collects and marshals impressions, mostly pessimistic, but he is often enough in doubt about his own wisdom. Sammler likes to stand on the moral high ground, but his doubt is what makes for his stature. At the end of the novel it is even possible to say that he is more wrong than right, and therefore a better man than we had thought, more loving and more obligated. For *Sammler* is a novel about obligation, and about the love that goes along with being obligated.

Sammler's style, mandarin, detached, and professorial, clearly owed much to Shils. Though Shils's biography differs vastly from Sammler's, it is clear that Bellow was working through his relationship with Shils in the novel. In the end, *Sammler* represents a quarrel with Shils much more than an endorsement. Bellow's Sammler gets shaken out of his theorizing, his arm's-length way of fending off the chaos that surrounds him. By the book's conclusion he no longer looks down on people—he looks at them. Remarkably, Bellow is able to make this shift in Sammler occur without sentimentality.

That Shils was a sociologist is important to Bellow. By dunking Sammler so thoroughly in the mad social reality of his time, Bellow argues that a novelist can do something that a sociologist simply can't. The novelist gravitates toward the chaos that sociology tries to tame and categorize. Novels give disorder a voice, letting us hear our own strange or hidden thoughts. A novelist's picture of a place and time is usually freer and more intimate than anything we can find in a work of sociology, because the novelist understands what the more abstract-minded sociologist misses—the role of personality.

The sixties provide a perfect stage for the fight between the world in the streets and the intellectual. Sammler, like Shils, maintains his distance from the arrogant forces of disorder. But finally Bellow makes Sammler reckon with the people around him. Unreasonable and off-kilter, the characters who surround Sammler refuse to conform to intellectual categories. Their very flaws make them worthy of being loved, Sammler sees. Sammler passes the test; Shils, to Bellow's mind, failed it. This is Bellow's trick on the intellectual type: trap him in life and see what happens. Shils remained aloof, refusing to be captivated by Bellow's key value, personality.

Shils, who was the son of a cigar maker, grew up in Philadelphia. On Sundays when he was a teenager he would leave the house in late morning and stay away until dinner-time, wandering through the city, drinking in its sights and sounds. These tours through Philadelphia's human cityscape, its crowded reality from the poor scrambling ghettos of the North Side to the manicured wealth of Rittenhouse Square, primed Shils to become a sociologist. As a student at Penn and then the University of Chicago, he fell hard for the theories of Max Weber and Georg Simmel, though his BA was in French literature rather than sociology. He became a social worker in 1930s Chicago, responsible for about eight hundred black families (throughout his life Shils was an ardent supporter of civil rights). After serving with the OSS in World War II, he returned to Chicago, where he resumed his career at the U. of C.

From his college years on, Shils sharply distrusted communism. "How could one have any respect for a movement so crudely unrealistic, untruthful, and manipulative?" he asked. He was nevertheless well-known to the Trotskyist clique at Chicago, which included Bellow and his friends Harold "Cappy" Kaplan, Herbert Passin, Isaac Rosenfeld, Lionel Abel, and Ithiel Pool. (During Bellow's time in Mexico, Al Glotzer, one of Trotsky's bodyguards, promised Bellow and Passin a meeting with "the old man," but they arrived a day too late, and saw Trotsky's bloody, bandaged body in the morgue.) "I thought they were rather foolish in their political and social views," Shils said of the Trotskyists, "but in their general culture and cleverness they were many cuts above the Stalinists." It was hard to resist the Trotskyists' energy, their strong appetite for ideas, their skill at debate. But Shils took their make-believe notions about proletarian revolution with a large grain of salt. It's worth noting that Shils also denounced McCarthyism in his brilliant 1956 book *The Torment of Secrecy*. He was as suspicious of right-wing as he was of left-wing manipulators.

Joseph Epstein remembers Bellow asking him in 1973, "Do you know any intelligent people in this city?" and adding that he himself knew three: Harold Rosenberg, David Grene, and Edward Shils, all members of the Committee on Social Thought. Epstein says he then knew Shils for his reputation as "a very formidable figure, distinctly not a man to fool with." (Alexandra Ionescu Tulcea Bellow, who was married to Bellow near the end of his friendship with Shils, told me that Shils "did his homework very thoroughly, he knew things about you that you wouldn't dream of . . . he was tough, he was very tough.") When Epstein finally met Shils sometime later, he discovered a paunchy, florid-faced professor wearing an old tweed jacket. Shils had an odd concocted accent, half Philadelphia and half Oxbridge, and, remarked Epstein, "a pronunciation system of his own devising." When he came to your house, the first thing Shils would do was inspect the books on your shelves. He delighted in mixing obscure Yiddish terms into his English sentences. Epstein remembers Shils emerging with him from a chili joint one afternoon. Pointing to some dangerous-looking young men, Shils remarked, "Joseph, note those three *shlumgazim*." Shils then had to explain to the baffled Epstein that "*Shlumgazim* . . . are highwaymen who, after stealing your purse, for sheer malice also slice off your testicles."

"He loved America, with all its philistinism and coarseness," Epstein wrote about Shils. But Shils also spent much time in Europe and consciously Europeanized his manners. He knew India well, too, and visited there often; he wrote about Indian intellectual life with sympathy and vividness. In his later years Shils lived in two homes, one in Chicago and one in Cambridge, England. In Chicago he had fifteen thousand books, all categorized precisely, library style. There were books everywhere you turned, floor to ceiling, along with busts of Joseph Conrad and Max Weber. Shils was a great reader of novels. The lover of Conrad, Dickens, and George Eliot never turned on the radio, and refused to own a television. Epstein, who replaced Bellow as Shils's best friend, brought Shils bags of magazines, allowing him to keep up with contemporary culture ("what the dogs [are] up to," as Shils put it). Shils's wit was rapier-sharp, and he delighted in deflating reputations. He made clear his low opinion of one colleague by saying, "I fear he believes Richard Rorty is a deep thinker" (Rorty had a notably smooth, folksy style, unusual for a philosopher, and the polar opposite of Shils's). Of a certain backstabbing professor, Shils noted that his specialty was putting bullets in other men's guns.

Shils could be brash in conversation. Epstein remembers introducing him in the seventies to the journalist Henry Fairlie. Shils said, "Mr. Fairlie, you wrote some brilliant things in the fifties. Now, I hear you have become a socialist. Please explain yourself." Fairlie, having had a few drinks, was more amused than offended. As editor of the academic journal *Minerva*, Shils said, "I take the leather whip to my contributors, but it doesn't seem to matter. They have steel bottoms." In his last years at Chicago, Shils had few friends among his colleagues except for Arnaldo Momigliano, a brilliant polymathic Italian-Jewish scholar. The long divorced Shils moved Momigliano into his apartment and took devoted care of him during Momigliano's lengthy final illness.

Shils shared with Bellow not just his origin as an intellectually ambitious working-class Jew, but much else too. Both had a fiercely independent habit of thought, and both exhibited a surprising facility in the kitchen (Shils, like Bellow, loved to cook for guests). Both had a talent for malice-laced wit, though Bellow, unlike Shils, occasionally had qualms about his sharp tongue (as in the story "Him with His Foot in His Mouth," which recalls, and regrets, a decades-old insult that Bellow directed at Irma Brandeis, a colleague at Bard). Shils, like Bellow, was generous with money—enormously so, in Shils's case, when a friend or a student needed help.

Most important, like Bellow, Shils seemed to notice everything and was capable of unlocking someone's personality with a single observation. In conversation Shils sometimes matched Bellow's own high, inventive language: he sounded like a novelist. Shils once said about Bellow that "he is a man who often laughs but in between seldom smiles." This is accurate and deeply telling: Shils shows something of Bellow's own skill at defining people. More than Bellow, though, he was an implacable judge of others and spoke with an impersonal, lofty authority that Bellow himself never attempted.

At the time that Epstein met him, Shils was still what Bellow called his "alter super-ego." But soon their friendship would fall to pieces. Decades later, after Shils's death, when Bellow wrote *Ravelstein*, he would devastatingly depict Shils as the short-fused, pitiless Rakhmiel Kogon, who is "high-handed, tyrannically fixated, opinionated. His mind was made up once and for all on hundreds of subjects," Bellow wrote. "His face wore a police expression and he often looked, walking fast, as if he were on a case." Kogon's notions of civility and decency, derived from Dickens, Burke, and Dr. Johnson, are overpowered by his "Weimar-style toughness." "He looked like a tyrant, with the tyranny baked into his face," Bellow remarked. And then the coup de grâce: Ravelstein insists that Kogon is attracted to men, while Chick, Bellow's narrator, refuses to believe he has any sexual life at all. In *Ravelstein* Bellow had his revenge on Shils by doing a Shils number on him. Without mercy Bellow clobbered his old friend turned enemy, who was just five years dead.

Shils's fondness for conventional authority had always put him at a certain distance from Bellow, the ex-Trotskyist and ex-Reichian. When he was Bellow's colleague at the Committee on Social Thought, Shils proved even more resistant to what he called sixties antinomianism than he had been to the communism of the thirties and forties. At the center of the antinomian temptation, he wrote, is "the emancipation of the individual from the burden of obligations." The rest of the creed, he declared with distaste, was that "charismatic authority is acceptable, but rational-legal or traditional authority is utterly repugnant," and that "all human beings are entitled to be gratified as the promptings of the self require."

The counterculture insisted that the realm of freedom was already beckoning to anyone willing to embrace it. To hear the beautiful young people tell it, perfect solutions to all social problems were readily available. "Youth is the sacred time of life," they chanted. But what the young rebels were actually doing was not sacred but tawdry, at times even fascistic, Shils darkly reported. Shils announced in print that President James Perkins of Cornell, "embracing the black students armed with revolvers" and agreeing to their demands, was comparable to Heidegger with his *Rektoratsrede* in praise of the Nazi regime. Disorder had hoisted its ragged pirate flag over America's finest universities, and Shils was appalled.

Shils prized the social bonds that were so rapidly fraying in the late sixties. The ebbing of solidarity troubled him deeply. What holds a society together? he asked. Shils found no answer in psychoanalysis, then a popular way to analyze social life. Psychoanalysis, he argued, did not explain or value human solidarity as it should. The superego could not speak in an intimate enough voice to cement the bonds among people. Freud's idea of authority made it look too threatening, Shils thought. In Freud's view authority works by making us afraid of it, instead of asking from us a reasonable, civilized obedience.

Shils believed that Freud was wrong. He knew that solidarity was strong and genuine, that it was founded on respect, obligation, humane impulse. Yet the sixties with its enthusiasm for disorder shook his confidence. The instinct to do as one liked had shattered the bonds of respect, and there seemed to be no way to put the broken world back together.

Shils's fear of the anarchy in the streets made him discount the attractions of rebellion. Bellow once remarked to Stanley Crouch that Dostoevsky had taught him something profound about how humans could become addicted to disorder. Shils was no Dostoevsky; he didn't want to understand the appeal of chaos. Shils's enthusiasm was for Conrad instead. Conrad insisted that we are and must be responsible for one another, but could not base his argument on anything more than our sense of duty. Neither could Shils, in the end. And so he was as incapable as Conrad would have been of sensing the true dimensions of the sixties revolt, with its cry that duty was at best an empty word, and at worst a blasphemy against the human spirit.

Bellow's friend John Berryman, in a letter to his mother, called *Mr. Sammler's Planet* "the wisest artwork of my generation so far." Berryman had long been a fire-breathing supporter of Bellow: when they taught together at Princeton he had read the manuscript of *Augie March* all weekend long, and then knocked on Bellow's window at four o'clock on Sunday morning to wake him up and tell him he'd written a masterpiece.

At times Bellow named *Sammler* as his own favorite

among his books. But he also voiced his doubts. "*Sammler* isn't even a novel," Bellow wrote in 1974 to Daniel Fuchs, a shrewd Bellow critic: "It's a dramatic essay of some sort, wrung from me by the crazy sixties." In his long interview with Norman Manea near the end of his life, Bellow remarked, "Where that book has intellectual content, the answers seem to me suspiciously easy." He had, he thought, fallen back on a prefabricated argument, an easy polemic against the chaos of the sixties. He was afraid, perhaps, that he resembled Shils, ready to denounce disorder without providing a viable remedy for it.

Bellow was too hard on himself. *Sammler* in fact stands as the closest thing to a perfect book that he made in his long writing career. It is symphonic in its vigor, efficient and spacious at once. It's also his most inflammatory novel, carefully designed to raise the reader's hackles. *Sammler* has been called reactionary, racist, and unforgivably unjust to the young. Flirting with the crudest of stereotypes, Bellow depicts an exhibitionist black pickpocket, whom he likens to a flamboyant, "barbarous-majestical" animal. Most notoriously, his Sammler attributes to the sixties counterculture the goal of "sexual niggerhood for everybody."

Bellow was not just playing with fire here, but openly shooting flames. Many years after the novel was published, the African American journalist Brent Staples revived the racial controversy over *Mr. Sammler's Planet* by following Bellow through his lakeside Chicago neighborhood, sporting with the distinguished man of letters by watching to see if he would quicken his step, afraid of the black man behind him. (Bellow's response when told of this was: Why didn't Staples just come and talk to me?) Stanley Crouch, who is also African American, defended Bellow in his preface to a reissue of the novel, pointing out the way Bellow attributes beastlike sexual oddity to a number of characters, not just the pickpocket. "Temporarily there is an animal emphasis" is Sammler's verdict on the sixties, and many of the book's people bear bestial traits. But they are also people with souls—no one is pure beast. Compassion wins out in *Sammler*, a novel that has been wrongly seen by many as strident, prejudiced, and weighted toward the reactionary.

Mr. Sammler's Planet is awash in the new humanity of the late sixties showing its exotic stripes, the whole scene played off against Artur Sammler, a man so much more than seventy, a Polish Jew and Holocaust survivor, highly polished in London before the war, and now living in New York. He is a remnant, a man out of time—like Shils, an Anglophile who adheres to the strict standards demolished by the sixties youth cult.

On the novel's first page Sammler opens his one good eye—the Nazis having long ago knocked out the other—on his spare Upper West Side bedroom. Considering the motley dirt-strewn city outside his window, he delivers a grand depressed reflection about the feeble nature of that "intellectual creature," "explaining man," who seeks "the roots of this, the causes of the other, the source of events, the history, the structure, the reasons why." Shils was, of course, as perfect an instance of explaining man as has ever lived; and Shils proved immune to Sammler's insight that "the soul wanted what it wanted," and "sat unhappily on superstructures of explanation, poor bird, not knowing which way to fly."

Unhappy with theories and reasons why, Sammler still spins out the theories and the reasons. But he knows that the soul, that poor bird, needs a perch in reality, a place of rest when the waters rise high.

Sammler is uncle to his nephew Elya, who is an old man like him, through a half sister. Elya has two children, Angela and Wallace. The cousins Shula and Angela, Sammler's daughter and Elya's, are both more than a little nutty. Shula's biggest stunt occurs when she steals the manuscript of a book about moon colonization written by Dr. Govinda Lal, an Indian mathematician. She aims to aid her father's research on H. G. Wells's plan for lunar colonies, but Sammler is appalled by the theft, and frantically seeks to get the manuscript back to Lal. At her best, toward the novel's end, the madly spirited Shula resembles a screwball heroine of the thirties.

Chapter One of *Sammler* centers on two iconic scenes, impossible to forget for any reader of the book. The first is based on an experience of Bellow's own, when, wearing an expensive suit, he delivered a lecture at San Francisco State in 1968 and was heckled by the writer Floyd Salas. Salas admired Bellow's books but felt crushed by the fact that Bellow had turned himself into an establishment man, a middle-aged eminence without a speck of sympathy for the student radicals. A beefy ex-boxer, Salas rose to his feet in the middle of Bellow's talk (titled "What Are Writers Doing in the Universities?") and reportedly proclaimed, "You're a fucking square. You're full of shit. You're an old man, Bellow." "So I left the platform in defeat," Bellow wrote to a friend, the writer Mark Harris, having been "denounced by Salas as an old shit to an assembly which seemed to find the whole thing deliciously thrilling."

Floyd Salas's attack on Bellow becomes an even more brutal spectacle in *Mr. Sammler's Planet.* The dignified and aloof Sammler is giving a lecture at Columbia about H. G. Wells. Suddenly a question bursts from one "thick-bearded" audience member: "Old Man! You quoted Orwell before. . . . Did Orwell say that British radicals were protected by the Royal Navy?" After Sammler's mild reply, "Yes, I believe he did say that," the heckler hurls at him a humiliating taunt, infantile-bravura in the manner of the late sixties:

> "That's a lot of shit."
>
> Sammler could not speak.
>
> "Orwell was a sick counterrevolutionary. It's good he died when he did. And what you are saying is shit." Turning to the audience, extending violent arms and raising his palms like a Greek dancer, he said, "Why do you listen to this effete old shit? What has he got to tell you? His balls are dry. He's dead. He can't come."

For a bare moment, with his Greek dancer's gesture, this hairy Dionysus touches smartass elegance. But all the rest is crude, and cruel. Chanting *shit, shit,* he wallows in the thoughtless splurge of the youth movement with its "confused sex-excrement-militancy," its "Barbary ape howling," as Sammler calls it. Tolerant, liberal Orwell has become anathema now. The heckler silences Sammler, who stops his lecture, and a sympathetic young girl leads him from the auditorium. "What a pity! Old Sammler thought. A human being, valuing himself for the right reasons, has and restores order, authority." But this mob will never show right reason. "Who had raised the diaper flag? Who had made shit a sacrament?" Outwardly composed, but with a prophet's rage burning inside him, Sammler gets on the downtown bus to go back home.

Then comes Bellow's second unforgettable scene. Sammler has for some time been watching a haut-dandy black pickpocket who works the bus near Columbus Circle, "a powerful Negro in a camel's hair coat, dressed with extraordinary elegance": Christian Dior shades, homburg hat, salmon-hued silk tie. During Sammler's bus ride down the West Side from his aborted lecture, the pickpocket, who realizes he's been seen in the act, decides to give Sammler a warning. Cool, unruffled, the towering, puma-like black thief follows Sammler off the bus and tracks him to the lobby of his apartment building. There he unveils his penis to the mesmerized old man:

> The pickpocket unbuttoned himself. Sammler heard the zipper descend. Then the smoked glasses were removed from Sammler's face and dropped on the table. He was directed, silently, to look downward.

> The black man had opened his fly and taken out his penis. It was displayed to Sammler with great oval testicles, a large tan-and-purple uncircumcised thing—a tube, a snake. . . . The man's expression was not directly menacing but oddly, serenely masterful. The thing was shown with mystifying certitude.

The refined, powerfully silent pickpocket and the ragged hippie protestor join together in their claim that the key is sex: that life force undeniable, asking obeisance. "We hold this, man, to be self-evident": so Sammler imagines the bold new declaration. That memorable black penis, the "huge piece of sex flesh, half-tumescent in its pride," haunts the novel. But the thief is nothing but splendid appearance. His famous dingus is not the thing itself, not power become flesh, but a paltry shadow.

Bellow's *Sammler*, with its suspicion of the overdressed will-to-power acted out by the black criminal, reads like a riposte to Norman Mailer's influential essay "The White Negro," published in 1957 in *Dissent*. In a presage of the sixties, Mailer said that the white hipster had absorbed the primitive energy of black America. Mailer celebrated "hip, which would return us to ourselves, at no matter what price in individual violence," and give us "an affirmation of the barbarian." Hip, he explained, proposes that "every social restraint and category be removed." Hipsters resemble psychopaths, Mailer argued, and "psychopathology is most prevalent with the Negro." He went on, "The psychopath murders—if he has the courage—out of the necessity to purge his violence." In the most notorious passage of his polemic Mailer announced that when "two strong eighteen-year-old hoodlums . . . beat in the brains of a candy-store keeper," this brutal killing is really a way of "daring the unknown." Mailer's brave criminal Negro has existential panache; Bellow's pickpocket, mere emptiness: he never says a thing. He is just one among the Dionysian horde in the streets, those "Hollywood extras" with their "imitative anarchy," "these Chinese revolutionary tunics, these babes in unisex toyland, these surrealist warchiefs, Western stagecoach drivers."

In his 1952 review of Ellison's *Invisible Man*, Bellow commented, "It is thought that Negroes and other minority people, kept under in the great status battle, are in the instinct cellar of dark enjoyment. This imagined enjoyment provokes envious rage and murder; and then it is a large portion of human nature itself which becomes the fugitive murderously pursued." Years before Mailer endorsed it, Bellow had already rejected the notion that blacks are, as he so precisely put it, "in the instinct cellar of dark enjoyment." The primitive and the sophisticated cohabit in black America as they do anywhere else, Bellow added. It is not just racist, but dangerous, even "murderous," to think otherwise. Bellow's black man, unlike Mailer's, is no catharsis-seeking psychopath. Shils too attacked the facile celebration of African Americans' desperate conditions by writers like Mailer when he wrote that, in the sixties, "blacks, according to this view, were entitled to exemption from the obligations of law-abidingness and of assimilation of the higher culture of

American and Western society. They gained merit from the fact that they lived in slums, in wretched dwellings." Like Bellow, Shils spoke out against such easy romanticizing of the wretched of the earth.

Artur Sammler's history leaves no room for romanticizing. He has survived the worst, crawling from a mass death pit in Poland, where he huddled next to the corpse of his wife until the Germans left. He is also a murderer, and he has enjoyed murder. But unlike Mailer, Sammler realizes it is mad to celebrate murder, to think of it as a wished-for freedom.

In the Polish woods, a famished half-human wreck, Sammler the partisan—"freezing, the dead eye like a ball of ice in his head"—carrying a gun, desperate, chewing grass and roots to keep alive, comes upon a German soldier. Sammler orders the German to strip: coat, sweater, socks, boots. In a low voice, the German pleads for his life. Without faltering Sammler shoots him twice, takes his bread, his gun, his clothes. "You would call it a dark action?" he muses to himself so many years later. "On the contrary, it was also a bright one. It was mainly bright. When he fired his gun, Sammler, himself nearly a corpse, burst into life. . . . His heart felt lined with brilliant, rapturous satin. To kill the man and to kill him without pity, for he was dispensed from pity."

Sammler needed to kill to come back to life, to wake up. Taking life is "one of the luxuries," he grimly decides. Stalin too, he thinks, must have experienced "that mighty enjoyment of consuming the breath of men's nostrils, swallowing their faces like a Saturn." Goya's shocking scene of Saturn devouring his children with vast, gruesome delight haunted Bellow; he mentions it again in *The Dean's December.*

No wonder that, when Sammler's niece Margotte gives him a lecture about the banality of evil, he scorns Hannah Arendt's famous theory. Sammler knows that the Nazis relished murder, and merely disguised it as banality. Here Sammler reflects Bellow's own view: he thought the Nazis fooled the strident, gullible Arendt, whom Bellow in a letter once called "that superior Krautess." The Germans of the Third Reich were no dutiful robots, but packed with vicious life.

Sammler meditates powerfully on the Nazi sense of humor, that high amused sadism with its "harshness toward clumsy pretensions, toward the bad joke of the self which we all feel." To the Nazi eye, Jewish morality was mere conceit, a thing comically easy for a man with a gun to demolish. You call this the king of the Jews? the Germans crowed. A filthy, mauled one begging for life? This dignified and learned man, this rabbi kicked and beaten, set on fire in front of his children? The Holocaust was the most consequential joke ever told.

In his many sociological writings, Shils gave scant attention to the role of violence. Bellow redresses the balance in *Sammler.* Rushing to see Elya at the hospital before he dies, Sammler notices a fierce fight in the street near Columbus Circle, with a crowd gathered around to watch. The black pickpocket, enormously tall, in alligator shoes, with matching crimson belt and necktie ("How consciousness was lashed by such a fact!"), is throttling a man named Lionel Feffer. This Feffer, now gasping for his life, holds a tiny Minolta. He has gotten the pickpocket on film, caught him in the act.

Sammler appeals to the crowd: "Some of you. . . . Break this up." He is met with silence, with the realization that "'some of you' did not exist." No solidarity, no bond: the facts of ordered society that Shils cherished are missing. And so Sammler's son-in-law, Eisen, steps in. Eisen is a veteran of Stalingrad, an Israeli metalworker and sculptor. He slams the pickpocket brutally with his bag of iron sculptures, and comes close to killing him. "Everything went into that blow, discipline, murderousness, everything," thinks Sammler with horror. The black man's face is gashed, swelling, crushed looking; and now Eisen prepares for his second blow. Eisen explains this to Sammler (for he is yet another explainer, in a novel full of them). "You can't hit a man like this just once. When you hit him you must really hit him. Otherwise he'll kill you. . . . If in—in. No? If out—out. Yes? No? So answer." These are words from Stalingrad, to which Sammler has no reasoned answer.

Responsibility steps in where reason cannot. Doing what one ought, that Hebraic theme, is worked deeply into *Sammler*'s ending. After Eisen, Sammler's second trial occurs in the hospital where Elya lies dying, and like the face-off with Eisen it concerns obligation. Elya knows his death is coming very soon. He learns that Angela is on her way to the hospital, and so he does a remarkable thing. He asks to be taken out of his room for tests, so that his daughter will not have to see him die.

At this very moment, in the hospital visitors' lounge, Sammler is having a disastrous quarrel with Angela. He wants Angela to apologize to her father for her reckless behavior with men. This is a deeply wrong move on Sammler's part. Indignant, wounded, Angela accuses Sammler of wanting "an old-time deathbed scene," a piece of moral playacting. When he finds out what Elya has done to exempt her from such an encounter, that he has died alone, unwilling to make his daughter suffer his, and her, debt of last words, Sammler knows he has sinned with Angela. He realizes that Elya's instinct to spare Angela was the right one, far better than Sammler's own wish to make her play the penitent. Out of disappointed love, but love nonetheless, Elya has let her go, at the same time that he himself lets go of life.

When he described Elya's choice to die alone, Bellow did something that Shils the rule-bound sociologist could never imagine. Shils and Bellow agreed on the crucial importance of obligation, but Shils never recognized the intimate form it could take. For him it was not part of the Old System, Bellow's family matrix, but rather a kind of societal glue. Ironically, perhaps fittingly, the dying Shils would end up rejecting a deathbed scene with Bellow when he refused to see and forgive him in his final days.

On the last page of Bellow's novel we finally hear Sammler pray. We know that he prays, for he has mentioned it several times, but now we hear him, and with force, as he remembers Elya: "At his best this man was much kinder than at my very best I have ever been or could ever be. He was aware that he must meet, and he did meet . . . the terms of his contract. The terms which, in his inmost heart, each man knows. As I know mine. As all know. For that is the truth of it—that we all know, God, that we know, that we know, we know, we know."

Solidarity starts to dawn in *Sammler*'s closing, the real thing this time, not the loose sixties notion: the "we" in "we know." "I want, I want" were the words that gnawed at Henderson. Tommy Wilhelm sobbed for everyone, but mainly for himself. But Sammler mourns with faith, because he is certain that we know what is required of us. And the members of his family—who else?—givers and takers all, are the ones who do the requiring.

The terms of Sammler's contract are clear: to know others with compassion, and to remember. Memories tell us who we are, as Freud taught, but they do more. They demand from us a just report, an account of the human integer, the loved person. They unseal the judgment. To sum up our memories of someone like Elya, and to reach a judgment about him, is to honor the contract.

THE POLITICAL LESSON of *Sammler* may seem at first glance to be something like Shils's claim that "liberals would sooner see their society ruined than learn something valuable to its preservation from conservatism." But Bellow remains in the end unconvinced by Shils's main message, that solidarity depends on tradition, authority, and adherence to civilized rules. For Bellow only conviction counts. The rescue from pessimism's dead end comes via the individual soul, not the sociologist's communal norms. What we owe, and how much, we ourselves know from the inside; no one else can tell us.

Mr. Sammler's Planet imposes its test on the old more than the young. Critics have complained that Bellow in *Sammler* derides the youth-worshipping decade of the sixties, but they have neglected the most heartfelt feature of the novel: Bellow's insistence that the aged Sammler must also stand trial. Sammler compares himself to Elya in his treatment of Angela, and finds that he falls short. The human lesson of Sammler goes far beyond liberal and conservative, old and young. Bellow tells us that our habits of judging will themselves be judged. No imagined moon colony, and no youth culture carnival, can transport us away from our knowledge of ourselves. The blackest history lurks in such knowledge, but love is there too.

CHAPTER 6

Delmore Schwartz

"THE PROUD and regal name Delmore," sang Lou Reed on one of his mournful solo albums, *The Blue Mask*. Reed was honoring his favorite teacher Delmore Schwartz, who by the early sixties, when he taught Reed at Syracuse University, had become a shambling wreck, wearing a torn overcoat smeared with toothpaste and capable of leaving the house with only one shoe. Years earlier he had slouched, as he put it, from "*il faut tenter de vivre*" to "*il faut* get out of the pajamas every other day." Delmore popped handfuls of Dexedrine as he sat in the Orange Bar, a popular Syracuse hangout, encircled by students: now spinning a bedraggled story about the Rockefellers, who had, he said, abducted his wife, now denouncing his endless turncoat friends, for instance his old pal Saul Bellow. Saul had raised money for him and then taken it all back, stipulating that the cash was to be used only for a stay in Payne Whitney, the high-class sanatorium where, Delmore's friends hoped, he would somehow piece himself together. At the Orange Bar, Delmore spoke to his disciples with rapture about everything from the New York Giants to Heinrich Heine, Buffalo Bill, and the sex life of T. S. Eliot. "Dwight [Macdonald] cheated him out of a house, Saul withheld money": so John Berryman, another of America's lost *poètes maudits*, recited Delmore's woes in one of the Dream Songs he dedicated to "the sacred memory of Delmore Schwartz."

In January 1966 Delmore abruptly left Syracuse and the last of a series of long-suffering student girlfriends and returned for his last few months of life to a seedy hotel in New York, where he read the tabloids and *Finnegans Wake*, drank his gin from a jar in the morning, and went out only to slurp soup at a deli counter or hunch warily over the bar at Cavanagh's, the old-time Irish saloon on Twenty-Third Street long ago favored by Diamond Jim Brady and the Tammany Hall crew. Delmore died on July 11, 1966, at the age of fifty-two of a heart attack in the corridor of the Columbia Hotel, trying to take out the trash.

"His mission was obscure. His mission was real, / But obscure," wrote Berryman about Delmore. And Bellow knew more about Delmore's mission than anyone. Delmore the kind, handsome, noble, crazy, illuminated, in spite of his mad vindictive streak the best-loved presence among the New York intellectuals, the one among them who stood perfectly for the artist, the dreamer, the man of mind and heart, all this about Delmore came through in Bellow's superb novel *Humboldt's Gift*, published in 1975. Delmore figures in Bellow's book as Von Humboldt Fleisher, the beautiful young poet and intellectual rhapsodist who eventually, beset by black paranoia, becomes a drug- and alcohol-addled conspiracy-monger. In the novel's opening pages Humboldt casts his spell on Charlie Citrine, an upward-hoping fledgling writer from Appleton, Wisconsin, Harry Houdini's hometown, who has just landed in New York: Charlie is Bellow's narrator and a clear stand-in for the author.

Bellow starts his book with a bright portrait of Humboldt. Charlie takes the ferry with Humboldt to Hoboken, where they eat steamed clams, drink beer, and smell the river breeze, and where Humboldt delivers to Charlie the first of many wide-swinging monologues. Frantic, hopped-up, Humboldt covers what seems like the whole history of the world. Just listen to this aria, as Charlie reports it: "His spiel took in Freud, Heine, Wagner, Goethe in Italy, Lenin's dead brother, Wild Bill Hickok's costumes, the New York Giants, Ring Lardner on grand opera, Swinburne on flagellation, and John D. Rockefeller on religion."

Humboldt is obsessed with the Abishag motif, the fall from grace to depravity, stardom to poverty; he too will fall on grim hard times, a spurned Hurstwood out of *Sister Carrie*. He says of Mae Murray, "She starred in *The Queen of Tasmania* and *Circe the Enchantress*, but she ended as a poorhouse crone." Even worse, there is "what's-his-name who killed himself in the hospital[.] He took a fork and hammered it into his heart with the heel of his shoe, poor fellow!" (Humboldt is thinking of the silent-film star Lou Tellegen, who stabbed himself to death with a pair of scissors in Hollywood's Cudahy Mansion.)

Bellow plucked the name Humboldt for his hero from the annals of European *Wissenschaft*, but also from Humboldt Park, his immigrant neighborhood in Chicago. As with Humboldt, everyone knew Delmore Schwartz by the high-toned first name his mother had picked for him. From time to time he claimed that his mother got the idea to call him Delmore from the sign on a delicatessen across the street from his house, but in fact Rose Schwartz had borrowed it from a neighboring family whose son was also a Delmore: such a beautiful name, she said.

Even in his last years, Delmore still had a noble spark, he was still from time to time the young man who had stunned the New York intellectuals with a quietly ravishing short story, "In Dreams Begin Responsibilities," written when he was twenty-one and featured in the first issue of *Partisan Review*, in the fall of 1937. Delmore's story opened the issue, before Edmund Wilson and Lionel Trilling, before Picasso and James T. Farrell and Mary McCarthy, before Wallace Stevens and James Agee. Delmore was on his way, and he knew it, cutting his bright swath, heralded so young as a talent who might even rival the modernist colossi.

"In Dreams Begin Responsibilities," though a work of fiction, tells Delmore's own story. Delmore's father, a hard-boiled, cynical gambler, left the family when the boy was nine, and so Delmore was raised by an overbearing mother whose love and resentment were both suffocating. Rose followed Delmore and his brother to summer camp, but she also later hounded Delmore with demands that he pay her back for his college education. Delmore admired his lost father (turned by Bellow in *Humboldt's Gift* into a Jewish cowboy who rode with Pancho Villa in Mexico). But he was temperamentally much closer to his brooding, sensitive mother. The startling conceit of "In Dreams," which Delmore wrote in a fever of creativity during one summer night in July 1935, is that a young man goes to the movies and sees a film of his own parents' courtship. The soon-to-be couple stroll at Coney Island, pose for a photograph, visit a fortune-teller, and gaze at the blind, restless waves that foreshadow their bleak future. Close to the story's end, the young man in the movie theater, observing his mother and father, rises to his feet and shouts, "Don't do it. It's not too late to change your minds, both of you. Nothing good will come of it, only remorse, hatred, scandal, and two children whose characters are monstrous." Family scandal was a piercing memory for Delmore: in 1921, during one of his parents' separations, Delmore's mother took him, then seven years old, by the hand and strode into a roadhouse restaurant. There she surprised Harry Schwartz with another woman, whom she denounced as a whore.

When "In Dreams Begin Responsibilities" appeared, Delmore was saluted as a new master. Years later, Vladimir Nabokov quietly asserted that "In Dreams" was one of his favorite stories, a rare occasion on which Nabokov praised a living author. One can see why: the story has a Nabokov-like irony wrapped around a flat but finely crafted prose style. Yet "In Dreams" never displays the connoisseur's grace with which Nabokov treats fate. The story depicts instead the most dire and inescapable destiny, and the most ordinary one, too: being born in just this way to just these people.

The photos of Delmore that came out in *Vogue* after his first book was published in 1938 show an electrically handsome, inspired-looking bard. In one, Greek-god-like, he poses with a Hellenic bust; in another, smoldering Byronically, he gazes into a mirror with "the eye of a Mongol horseman," as Robert Lowell wrote in a sonnet about Delmore. Delmore made his mark on the literary world before Lowell's and Randall Jarrell's obsession with childhood, before Berryman's self-lacerating ego, before Sylvia Plath's suicidal glamor. The precarious narcissistic grandeur of these later poets, all of them except Plath friends of Delmore, was inspired in part by him, their elder brother.

"In Dreams" shows Delmore's bondage to the heavy weight of the past. More and more as the years went by, Delmore was disastrously obsessed by Freud, convinced he could never win the family struggle, that everything had been determined from before his own birth. The epic autobiographical poem he completed in 1942, called *Genesis*, was a hopeless excursion into the family romance; a nervous mock-solemnity mars the book. Delmore considered *Genesis* his masterpiece, but the critics didn't agree. For them, he was a once promising young man who had floundered, sunk by the idea that his parents' doomed marriage had once and for all sealed his fate.

In *Genesis*, Delmore was riffling through the details of his past, searching desperately for the answer to the riddle of his character, which was sometimes melancholy and idealizing, sometimes pulsing with manic life. But however much he sought the origins of his self in his childhood memories, he could never recover his creative spark. He was a lost soul, convinced of his failure, and his rebellion against the successful ones—against people like Bellow—turned more bitter and helpless as the years passed. He was galvanized by gossip and rumor, and could be conniving, gloating, vengeful. When Mary McCarthy left Philip Rahv for Edmund Wilson in 1937, Delmore's biographer James Atlas writes, this was "a development Delmore dwelled on with great exuberance." Delmore disliked Rahv, about whom he quipped, Oscar Wilde style, "Philip has scruples, but he never lets them stand in his way." But he also enraged Wilson, along with everyone else who had helped his career. Delmore's fantasies about people with power, money, and success turned out-and-out crazy, and his urge to pick fights ensured his isolation. One friend after another disappeared, disheartened by Delmore's accusations. Drugs were becoming a problem, too, and the problem would get worse. "Just before eating a small lunch, five, six, seven, eight Dex" is a typical Delmore journal entry from the fifties, when he headed more steeply downward.

Among the New York intellectuals Delmore had no closer friend than William Barrett, an Irish working-class boy who quickly assimilated to the nervous energy of the Jewish thought-mavens in the *Partisan Review* crowd. Barrett remarked on Delmore's "curious hop, as if he couldn't stand still with glee, his arms flapping against his sides like a chicken's wings." Delmore's original gaiety enthralled his friends, but as time went on his energy turned manic, uncontrollable. While lecturing at Columbia in 1948 on "The Literary Dictatorship of T. S. Eliot," Delmore drank a tumbler of straight gin to settle his nerves. He was auditioning for a teaching position, but Trilling, aware of Delmore's erratic behavior, nixed the appointment.

Bellow met and got to know Delmore sometime in the late forties, during one of his trips to New York. In 1944 Delmore praised *Dangling Man*, Bellow's first novel. By 1952 he had secured one-year teaching positions for both himself and Bellow at Princeton: Delmore was in his hopped-up, plotting phase. In *Partisan Review* Delmore claimed that *Augie March* was better than *Huckleberry Finn.* In a 1954 letter to Sam Freifeld, Bellow described Delmore as "my strange delightful buddy." By October 1957, he was writing to James Laughlin, "About Delmore, I'm just as depressed as you are. He's got it in his mind that I'm one of his ill-wishers . . . and he phoned me in the middle of the night using techniques the GPU might have envied." Delmore, convinced that Hilton Kramer was having an affair with his wife, was equally sure that Bellow was in cahoots with Kramer; he put a private detective on Bellow's tail. The relationship between the two men would not recover. In *Humboldt's Gift*, Bellow honors Delmore by looking back at him, and taking a loving, battered view of both the bold inspired young poet and the distracted middle-aged wreck.

Humboldt's Gift is a pure romp, a tremendous achievement for a book about sex, death, madness, and money. It is more than anything else a comic novel. *Humboldt*'s first hundred pages are a whirlwind, a virtuoso rapture that can rival anything in American literature for gusto. The comedy comes from the antic spirit of Humboldt, but also from Charlie Citrine, the Bellow character. Charlie is realist enough to reject Humboldt's enraptured delusions, but he himself has Rudolf Steiner–spurred dreams of surmounting mortality. (After his Reichian enthusiasm ebbed, Bellow became a Steiner fan.) Charlie is aware of his own ridiculousness, both in amorous matters—Renata, a voluptuous younger woman, holds him captive—and in his eccentric methods of self-help. Standing on his head in the only yoga position he knows after his Mercedes has been smashed to pieces by a thug, Charlie courts a lighter brand of absurdity than the one the modernist mythmakers endorsed. In *Humboldt's Gift* no abysses are stared into, but the novel is for all its loony touches a work of high seriousness.

Bellow is at his most serious in *Humboldt* when he shows how Humboldt, the high-dreaming bard, mistakenly sees a kind of beauty in fame, influence, and money. (Charlie is susceptible to this gospel too.) Humboldt wants real worldly power, and in this he echoes Delmore. When Adlai Stevenson ran against Eisenhower in 1952, Delmore, stirred with excitement, said he had it on very good authority that Stevenson was reading his poems on the campaign trail. Stevenson was going to make it to the White House, Delmore insisted in hushed tones, and then he would become Adlai's cultural advisor. Thus would bloom a new Weimar—but it was not to be. What came instead was dull, slumbering, anti-intellectual Ike.

Like Delmore, Humboldt was crestfallen after the dismal 1952 election returns, when Adlai lost to Ike by a wide margin. Humboldt hatches a new plot: to become professor of poetry at Princeton. If Humboldt cannot sway Washington, he can, he thinks, at least ascend to the top of the Ivy League heap. The added kick for him is that a Jew will get to infiltrate the WASP inner sanctum. Charlie goes to Princeton with Humboldt to secure English Department jobs for both of them.

This strand of Bellow's story is closely based on fact. In 1952 the influential critic R. P. Blackmur, a hard-drinking, loquacious poor boy who had climbed the ivory tower and become one of America's preeminent literary critics, was about to leave for a yearlong Fulbright in the Middle East. In *Humboldt's Gift*, a Professor Sewell, closely modeled on Blackmur, is similarly about to depart Princeton for a Fulbright in Damascus, and Humboldt proposes to replace him for a year. Charlie, Humboldt, and Sewell go to lunch together, and so the plot advances: Humboldt easily engineers a position for himself as Sewell's replacement, with Charlie in tow as his assistant. Charlie's line on Sewell is devastating: he sees in him "a muttering subtle drunken backward-leaning hollow-faced man," with sparse hair and a "dry-cereal" moustache, crossing his legs with spurious elegance. Sewell looks like the sterile butt-end of high modernism, a hollow man, headpiece filled with straw. Humboldt, by contrast, is full of ardent life, a drink from romantic springs.

Just as memorable as Humboldt is the gangster Rinaldo

Cantabile, who savages Charlie's treasured Mercedes. Cantabile cuts a major figure in *Humboldt's Gift*: "raging from the neck up," he is a mink-moustached, testosterone-piloted zany, a dandy in a raglan coat who matches Humboldt himself in kooky ardor, and whose bizarre ingenious plots outdo even Humboldt's. Another Bellovian reality instructor, he plays both Charlie's louche tormentor and his pal. Charlie has refused to give Cantabile his winnings from a poker game, since Cantabile was cheating (he is egged on by his bull-necked friend George Swiebel, based on Dave Peltz, who angrily shouts at him "No pay!"). So the gangster whacks Charlie's car to pieces. After Charlie crumples and gives Cantabile the money he owes him, Cantabile takes him up to a lofty construction site where he makes the terrified Charlie stalk gingerly from beam to beam. He sails Charlie's fifty-dollar bills from the shining steel girders far up in the air. *This is my temptation in the wilderness*, Charlie thinks. Many hundreds of feet high, unforgiving winds buffet these two aging boys, the writer and the hoodlum.

Cantabile bonds Charlie to him in outrageous ways. Suddenly needing to shit, he drags Charlie with him into the toilet stall at the Russian Baths on Division Street, cementing a fetid intimacy between the two men. Later, he proposes a ménage à trois. The emotional scuffling between Charlie and Cantabile leads to a cankered friendship: both have their labyrinthine soul struggles.

Charlie's gorgeous wrecked Mercedes, maimed by Cantabile's baseball bat, is a smashed love object, an image of fleshly vulnerability. The car's frailty resembles that of the body, and tells us that the proud, anxious ladies man Charlie, with his devotion to the gym and his will to keep his sex life going strong, has been fooling himself. He sees himself as a Marc Antony cruising the city with Renata, his Cleopatra, royally defying middle age. But the slow waning of life turns out to be more powerful than the hectic effort to keep up. *Humboldt's Gift* ends, after Charlie has lost Renata, in a recognition of age and death, and a clinging to the memory of the dead.

The most vivid character in *Humboldt*'s female cast list is the smart-talking, nervous Demmie Vonghel, Renata's forceful opposite number, based closely on Bellow's longtime girlfriend Maggie Staats. The ex-debutante Demmie is forthright, comforting, has bad dreams about hell, and is a whiz at cards. Like Shirley MacLaine in *The Apartment* pronouncing "shut up and deal," she growls to Charlie during a gin game, "I'm gonna clean you out, sucker." When Demmie sends Charlie off to his interview in Princeton, Bellow describes a marvel of tenderness: "In her cloth coat with the marten collar, with her sublime sexual knees that touched, and the pointed feet of a princess, and her dilated nostrils presented almost as emotionally as her eyes, and breathing with a certain hunger, she had kissed me with her warm face." Bellow makes Demmie die in a plane crash over South America. The real Maggie Staats lived on; for a time Bellow divided his affections between her and Arlette Landes, on whom he based his portrait of Renata.

Humboldt keeps his own beloved in purdah. Kathleen, based on Delmore's wife, the novelist Elizabeth Pollet, is

Humboldt's near captive in his decaying New Jersey house. Bellow depicts Kathleen as a sweet, out-of-tune companion to Humboldt, playing touch football with him in their yard in "Nowhere, New Jersey," then sitting by Humboldt and Charlie as they watch the late show, a Bela Lugosi horror movie about a mad scientist who creates synthetic flesh.

Here Bellow stays close to Delmore's biography. Delmore had bought a ramshackle home in New Jersey, far from the epicenter of New York and its cultural titans. There he shared his cornered existence with Elizabeth, who had become a best-selling novelist. Delmore's paranoid jealousy ballooned to epic proportions. In his wilder fits Delmore claimed that behind his back Elizabeth was having affairs with a host of strange men. Once Delmore dragged Elizabeth violently away from a Princeton party after she plucked a match from Ralph Ellison's pocket; he threw her into their car and drove recklessly, violently away. (This was the party that Bellow attended with Sondra Tschacbasov, already described in Chapter Four.) Bellow tells the tale of this bizarre, frightening night in *Humboldt's Gift*: Kathleen's shoes are left on the lawn, and the car winds up in a ditch.

As Humboldt declines, Charlie rises: so it was with Delmore and Bellow. Charlie becomes a famous man after the runaway success of his Broadway play, whose hero, named von Trenck, was, so Humboldt angrily thinks, based on him. Humboldt seethes: Charlie has exploited and betrayed him.

Humboldt's gallery of characters peaks in Bellow's courtroom scenes. Exhausting legal wars with Susan Glassman exercised Bellow during *Humboldt*'s writing. Susan's lawsuit claiming that he had underreported his income, which dragged through the courts for much of the seventies, seemed to Bellow surreally vindictive. (She won, eventually.) The battered Bellow took his literary revenge in *Humboldt's Gift*, where Denise's divorce lawyer is a showy brute, "cannibal Pinsker" in his loud, checked yellow suit and two-tone tan shoes. Cantabile gleefully tells Charlie about Pinsker: "Yiy! Pinsker, that man-eating kike! . . . He'll chop up your liver with egg and onion"—and so it turns out. In his courtroom scenes Bellow mightily skewers Susan's rapacity, as he saw it. He is reported to have said after one particularly draining courtroom session in 1971, "I watch her, and as a character in a novel she's delicious, but in real life she's a monster."

Humboldt ends with Menasha Klinger's aria at Humboldt's grave. Menasha was a boarder in Charlie's house when he was a kid. Even then, working as a punch-press operator, he had a bad, roosterish voice and the indefatigable yen to become an opera singer. Many decades later, Charlie visits Menasha and Humboldt's uncle Waldemar Wald at Coney Island, a poignant and hilarious scene that Roth leaned on for his portrait of Cousin Fish in *Sabbath's Theatre*. At the very end of *Humboldt's Gift* Waldemar and Menasha preside with Charlie over the reburial of Humboldt and his mother in Valhalla, a prestigious cemetery for German Jews. No one remembers the kaddish, or any other prayer for that matter, and so Menasha steps in and performs two songs, "In questa tomba oscura" from *Aida* and the old spiritual

"Goin' Home." Menasha clasps his hands and, "rising on his toes, and as emotionally as in our kitchen on Rice Street, weaker in voice, missing the tune still, and crowing but moved, terribly moved, he sang his aria."

Bellow picks for *Humboldt*'s closing note an old man with a long-ago-shot voice singing a Verdi aria in beautifully deluded, cracked style. This is off-kilter amateur ambition as the antidote to the grandiose Humboldt, and antidote too to Charlie's sorrow for his middle-aged self.

Menasha Klinger's aria clues us in that *Humboldt's Gift* aims to be what the critic Manny Farber called termite art. According to Farber in his 1962 essay "White Elephant Art vs. Termite Art," the termite artist rebels against "the idea of art as an expensive hunk of well-regulated area," and instead chews away with "eager, industrious, unkempt activity." The enemy of termite art is white elephant art, which is Farber's name for masterpiece art. The white elephant artist wants to "install every event, character, situation in a frieze of continuities": all too perfect, too just right.

Farber in his essay was concerned mostly with paintings and movies. He should have spent some time on novels, because novels more than any other form are naturally hospitable to termites. The nature of storytelling is to spill over, rush ahead, and get sidetracked. The novelist who tries to fill every nook with perfectly suitable detail has mistaken the character of the form, which dotes on the ragged. Dostoevsky is a termite artist par excellence. So is Dickens, another of Bellow's favorites. Bellow, in a radically different emotional key from Dostoevsky or Dickens, like them wants the looseness and the power that come from lack of order. He packs the ending of *Humboldt* with odd lightweight divagations: George Swiebel goes to Nairobi in search of beryllium, Pierre Thaxter gets captured by terrorists. (The dandyish Thaxter, based on Keith Botsford, is a curious cosmopolitan man of letters, looking like Puss in Boots with his blue velvet suit, his cloak, and his tilted-brim black hat, delighted by Chicago crooks, shifty with money, full of grandiose schemes.)

Termite artists refuse "the continuity, harmony, involved in constructing a masterpiece," Farber declares. They have their own kind of ambition: above all they refuse to get caught and sent to the zoo like the white elephant. What tripped up Delmore was the prestige of T. S. Eliot ("Uncle Tom," as he called him), who more than anyone else stood for white elephant art. Delmore's essays abound in judicious Eliotic rhetoric. He evaluates, discerns, pronounces judgment. But Eliot's high church outfit never really suited the psychically unkempt Delmore. Bellow's own judgment on Delmore's aloof high culture posturing comes near the end of *Humboldt's Gift*. Humboldt, he says, had made himself boring.

Humboldt's proclamations about art and culture run up a blind alley. His true forte turns out to be the termite art of the two rude, bizarre film treatments he bequeaths to Charlie, recounted by Bellow in a wild scherzo out of Preston Sturges. One treatment, which Charlie and Humboldt cooked up together during their Princeton days, concerns an Italian Arctic explorer reduced to cannibalism during a polar expedition. Back in Italy, he sells gelato to adoring schoolchildren under the name Signore Caldofreddo; the media discovers his tragic secret, but the townspeople forgive him. Crazily, the absurd Caldofreddo scenario gets turned into a movie and becomes a massive hit in Europe. Humboldt's other movie idea concerns a screenwriter who takes his mistress on a tropical vacation and turns the voyage into a screenplay—but not before retaking the same trip with his wife in a futile effort to quiet her suspicions, in a madcap riff on Kierkegaard's *Repetition*.

The fact that Bellow makes a place in his book for the two treatments, these strange and flimsy jeux d'esprit, shows that he values properly what was most remarkable in Delmore: not his ambition to write a great poem or to become an arbiter of culture, but his talent for throwaway gestures and antic tale-telling. By taking on Delmore's termite energy, Bellow was able to write *Humboldt's Gift*, the freest and the strangest among his many books.

In a letter to his publisher James Laughlin, Delmore recommended to him a French novel

> in which the hero is Thomas Alva Edison, who is very sad because he was born too late to make phonograph recordings of all the great sounds of history—the fall of Jericho, the Flood, the opening of the Red Sea, and the like[.] An Englishman in love with a very beautiful and very stupid opera singer commissions Edison to make a dummy automaton

> who looks just like the singer and sings like her, so that he will be free of his infatuation. Edison does, and the two ladies meet and it is all quite profound, in its way.

Termite art! There was, of course, no such novel. Delmore had made it all up, and it was Delmore all the way, just as demented as Bellow's tale of the old Italian cannibal.

In *Humboldt's Gift* Bellow marvelously describes Verlaine and Poincaré on their separate ways to lunch in fin-de-siècle Paris, "Verlaine drunken and bloated pounding his cane wildly on the sidewalk as he went to lunch, and shortly afterward the great mathematician Poincaré, respectably dressed and following his huge forehead while describing curves with his fingers, also on his way to lunch." Delmore was both these men, the sodden crazy Verlaine and, in his best poems, the beautifully precise Poincaré, a Platonic perfectionist. Bellow zeroed in on Delmore the wild character, who was in the end far more intriguing than the writing he could not sustain.

Shortly before Humboldt's death, Charlie glimpses the mad-eyed writer gnawing a pretzel stick on the street and darts away to avoid his gaze. These are Humboldt's "grim gorilla days," when he paces the cage of his sickness. Years later he remembers the "mad-rotten majesty" picture the *New York Times* chose to print beside its obituary of Humboldt. Here Bellow clearly nods to the famous photo of Delmore taken by Rollie McKenna: the poet sits on a bench in Washington Square Park, his gaze frantic and unsettled, at his feet a wind-blown copy of the *Daily News* with the headline "Heiress Keeps Her Millions." Delmore's thirst for high-society gossip stayed with him to the end, along with his need for great literature and for wild conspiracy theories. We do best to remember him, not in the megalomaniac glory of his youth, and not in his final bitter siege at the Columbia Hotel, but quietly absorbed, reading *Finnegans Wake* in his seat at the Polo Grounds, loyal to the Giants.

CHAPTER 7

Alexandra Ionescu Tulcea Bellow

BELLOW MARRIED AGAIN in 1974, this time to a woman who was the polar opposite of Susan Glassman: an academic with a taste for solitary work. Alexandra Ionescu Tulcea was a celebrated mathematician who taught at Northwestern. When she met Bellow at a party in 1973, she had no idea who he was. He said he wrote books, and she apologized that she hadn't read any of them. Bellow responded, "Well, I haven't read any of your books either." Then he asked her to name a book she'd written, and she said *Topics in the Theory of Lifting*. Both Saul and Alexandra liked to recite this meet-cute. At their first meeting, Alexandra told me, "suddenly he looked up at me and asked, 'How would you like to be my wife?' I was very taken aback, but much later I realized this was one of his opening lines with women he found attractive."

Saul and Alexandra were proud of their closeness, their special bond. One friend remembers them eating off the same plate at a dinner party. "He was everything that the mathematicians were not," Alexandra recalled. "One of the first things he taught me was that life is not really black and white; not every problem is solvable."

Alexandra taught Bellow as well. He asked her about mathematics, and even took a calculus course for a little while. She showed him a few basic proofs from Euclid. And she gave him to read *A Mathematician's Apology* by G. H. Hardy, a book he thought wonderful. Hardy was an English don whose math was reportedly as elegant as his writing. His *Apology*, which explains the lure of math to a nonmathematical audience, is a beautiful book. It is also a mournful one: Hardy, in his sixties when he wrote it, had lost his mathematical abilities. Few mathematicians achieve anything past sixty, and most reach their peak in their twenties or thirties. When Alexandra married Bellow, she was thirty-nine—twenty years younger than Bellow—and still labored tirelessly at her field. "Saul was a devil about work," she recalled; and so was she. But she feared that she would soon be too old to do major work in mathematics. Bellow must have been asking himself the same thing about his writing career: Would he ever again have the stamina for another five hundred pages like the wild, loose-limbed *Humboldt's Gift*?

Alexandra's fears of a creative drought proved to be unfounded. In the 1980s, during her marriage to Bellow, she made groundbreaking advances in an area of math called ergodic theory. She continued to do math, and write significant papers, even in her sixties. Decades earlier, she had done her work in collaboration with her first husband, in the feverish workaholic excitement that young mathematicians know so well. Now she remade her life with someone from the other side of the tracks: a writer.

Bellow's marriage to Alexandra lasted a little more than a decade. She incarnated a surprising otherworldliness that Bellow found himself drawn to in his sixties. She was the absentminded professor who liked to tap-dance on the porch of the house they lived in during summers in Vermont, girlishly charming and warm but intensely devoted to her work. Bellow's agent Harriet Wasserman remembers her saying quietly to herself "Yup, yup," working out a problem in her head while she flipped burgers for lunch.

Alexandra was born in Bucharest, the daughter of two doctors. Her mother was a child psychiatrist. Alexandra's father, Dumitru Bagdasar, was born the twelfth child in a Moldovan peasant family, but against all odds became a spectacularly innovative brain and spinal-cord surgeon. After a stint as a military doctor in World War I, where he almost died of typhus, he studied in Boston with the world-renowned Dr. Harvey Cushing. Cushing worked slowly, with excruciating care, determined to spare as much of the brain as he could. Bagdasar later described Cushing's operations: "They had something of the atmosphere of a sacred act, a severe, sustained ritual." Bagdasar was a brilliant pupil and Cushing took him under his wing. "You could have had a penthouse on Park Avenue," an American friend remarked, shaking his head at Bagdasar's decision to return to Romania. Bagdasar established a pioneering neurosurgical clinic in Bucharest and performed thousands of surgeries, during which he achieved near miracles. After one of his exhausting multihour brain operations, his wife joked, "Do you think Hades will be upset that you've stolen one of his subjects?"

Roza Samet Zaloziecki, a Jewish obstetrician and gynecologist, was hidden with Alexandra's family near the end of the war. (Roza's husband, Alexis Zaloziecki, also a famous neurologist, was, Alexandra wrote later, "a princely personality and a force of nature": when Alexandra and her new husband left Romania in 1957 he told them affectionately, "Get out and never come back.") On April 4, 1944, with American planes heavily bombing Bucharest, Alexandra's parents set out for the shelter, only to realize that Roza and her infant son weren't following them. They returned to find the baby still on the potty. This saved their lives: the shelter was destroyed that day, and everyone inside was killed. When the Bagdasars visited the shelter to give first aid, they were appalled by the carnage, with limbs strewn through the rubble and lakes of blood everywhere.

Alexandra's father was an ardent Communist during the war. Profoundly opposed to the Nazi barbarism, he welcomed a Soviet victory with open arms. The new regime named him ambassador to the United States. But by this time he was slowly dying of lung cancer. "The day when he realized he could not keep the knife in his hand was the saddest day of his life," Alexandra wrote many years later in a memoir of her parents.

When her father died in 1946, just as the Soviet Union was setting its iron grip on Romania, Alexandra was ten years old. That same year her mother, Florica Bagdasar, became Romania's minister of health. She had to confront typhus, famine, malaria: in the wake of the war Romania was devastated by disease. She fought hard against the Romanian government, which didn't want her to request American aid for the starving masses in Moldova—and she won. The American help came, the Red Cross distributed supplies, and the famine was stopped. But the regime did not forget Florica's defiance. By the end of 1947, Stalinism had taken full possession of Romania, and the next year Florica was fired as health minister, while the Stalinist press denounced the Marshall Plan's effort to "enslave" Eastern Europe with food aid—a clear slap in the face to the now embattled Florica.

Florica went on to head an innovative psychiatric clinic for children. But that ended in 1953, when the regime condemned her for corrupting working-class children with bourgeois ideas. Child psychology, especially if it drew on Freud, was now taboo. Such so-called science "demeans and slanders" man, the government announced, by distracting workers from the class struggle. Alexandra was in high school, and she found herself shunned by her classmates because of her mother's downfall. A few years later, as a result of Nikita Khrushchev's de-Stalinization, Florica was rehabilitated and even given permission to travel abroad. But the shock of her mother's disgrace had permanently marked Alexandra.

Alexandra attended the University of Bucharest and married a young professor in the Math Department, Cassius Ionescu Tulcea. He was invited to a research program at Yale in 1957, Alexandra came along, and they both defected. Their academic careers flourished: by the mid-sixties both were professors at Northwestern. The couple divorced in 1969, the same year that their book on lifting theory was published. Cassius went on in later years to write books on casino gambling, including craps and blackjack.

The Romanian regime allowed Alexandra's mother to visit her in Chicago several times during the two decades after Alexandra came to America. But Alexandra returned to Romania only in the weeks before Florica's death in 1978—the story Bellow retells in *The Dean's December.* Then, she would be treated as a traitor to the Romanian state and punished by being denied access to her dying mother.

In a 1984 interview with Bellow, D. J. R. Bruckner described Bellow's and Alexandra's apartment—or, rather, apartments. Bellow's writing studio, he reported, is

> A room thirteen floors above Lake Michigan at the east end of the long apartment that could give one a fit of geometric hallucination. In the 1970s, Bellow and his wife, Alexandra, bought two flats in the brick high-rise on Chicago's north side and cut a door into the wall separating them; they left the rest of the structure unchanged. From the doors the resulting apartment unfolds both ways, each half

a mirror image of the other. There are doubles of everything—baths, sets of bedrooms, living rooms, kitchens.

Alexandra's studio was at the distant end of their apartment, as far away from Bellow's as possible. In the morning, when he sat down to work, Bellow would open the curtains on his lakeside view and crank up Mozart on the stereo. "It was loud as can be," Alexandra remembered. "He would surround himself with sunshine and music. I, on the other hand, would close the door to my office and shut the curtains, because even the view of the lake and the beach was a distraction." Alexandra added that "early in the marriage I remembered Saul saying, 'Oh what a relief to have a woman who doesn't breathe down my neck, who has her own professional interests, and who lets me be all morning.'" But Bellow's gratefulness for the parallel lives that he and Alexandra led would later turn to resentment at what he saw as her coldness, her distance.

Bellow was careful to allow Alexandra her private space. In his 1984 interview he said, "You cannot believe how oblivious a mathematician becomes doing mathematics," but he added that he didn't play his violin in the Chicago apartment: "I am afraid that around here my scratching would be painful to Alexandra's ears."

IN 1976, the year after *Humboldt's Gift* was published, Bellow won the Nobel Prize. Only Americans won Nobels that year, and so at the prize ceremony a Swedish band, wearing eighteenth-century wigs, played tunes from *West Side Story*. "It was magical, it was like a whole week of fairy tale, this very young and handsome king and queen," Alexandra remembered. Sixteen Bellows traveled to Stockholm for the ceremony, including Bellow's brother Sam, who was about to go to federal prison for money laundering (though Sam had done nothing wrong, he took the rap for a relative). "How was Stockholm?" Bellow's friend Sam Goldberg asked him on his return. "Meshuga!" Bellow replied.

More than meshuga was Bellow's alimony trouble. Salary checks from the Committee on Social Thought were not keeping pace with Susan's demands. He later confessed that the Nobel money had gone directly into Susan's bank account.

Bellow's son Daniel had his coming of age during the trip to Stockholm for the Nobel ceremony. When I mentioned a photograph of Daniel between his two elder brothers, Greg and Adam, Daniel told me, "I was drunk for the first time in my life. That photo with the brothers—I'm in the middle because they're propping me up, I'm so drunk. I'm shit-faced, I'm twelve years old, and I'm looking for the queen so I can ask her to dance. I'm asking Adam, Where's the queen? It was my bar mitzvah. Pop taught me the lines from 'Minnie the Moocher': 'She had a dream about the king of Sweden / He gave her things that she was needin'.'"

Alexandra was the only non-Jew among Bellow's wives. But for the last few decades of his career he would become more and more interested in Jewish matters, especially when the fate of the Jews intersected with world politics. *To Jerusalem and Back* tells the story of Bellow's stay in Israel in 1975, recounting the conversations he had there about the Jewish people and the Jewish state. He sketches a loving portrait of Alexandra in the book: she was essential to his journey.

Alexandra was Bellow's ideal partner in his tour of Israel. She was a gentile without a trace of bad feeling toward Jews, open to experience and willing to be instructed. Decades later she remembered her time with Bellow in the Holy Land as one of the best periods of her life, full of social gatherings and friendship, the antithesis to grim Romania under communism. In Israel she visited her friend from childhood Roza Zaloziecki, then in her seventies and still a practicing obstetrician.

Both before and after she left Romania, Alexandra's political naïveté protected her to some extent. Bellow had to tell her about Stalin's crimes. Concentrated on her mathematics, she knew little about the NKVD or the Gulag. Now, she would plunge into a place where politics seemed like life itself.

On their 1975 trip to Israel, Alexandra lectured in mathematics at The Hebrew University of Jerusalem. Here she and Bellow met the Latvian mathematician Eliyahu Rips, a "very dramatic and heroic figure," Alexandra recalled. Rips embodied the solitary self-sufficiency of so many mathematicians, including Alexandra, but there was something dangerously extreme about him also, a fanatical integrity. In his Jerusalem book Bellow tells Rips's astonishing story: "When the Russians went into Czechoslovakia, Rips, a mathematics student, set himself on fire in protest. The flames were beaten out and Rips was sent to an insane asylum. While there, without books, he solved a famous problem in algebra."

Rips immigrated to Israel just before the Yom Kippur War, got a job at a gas station and, Bellow writes, "offered to work for nothing, feeling that he must make a contribution to Israel's defense. So for some months he pumped gas, unpaid." Eliyahu Rips was a living emblem of Jewish resurrection, like the country of Israel itself. "No people has to work so hard on so many levels as this one," Bellow observed.

In 1982 Bellow wrote *The Dean's December*, his gloomiest novel, based on his and Alexandra's 1978 trip to Romania, three years after their stay in Israel. Alexandra, here called Minna, provides a slate, steady light: she is the novel's anchor. Bellow's *Dean* is really, in spite of its bleak mood, a love poem for Alexandra, whose seeming absentmindedness hides an invisible and charming depth. "You might love a woman for her tactfulness alone," Albert Corde, the dean of the title, thinks about the subdued and tenacious Minna.

The Bucharest section of *The Dean's December* centers on Minna's effort to see her dying mother in the hospital. The Communist regime puts obstacles in her way designed to break her heart, and nearly succeeds. Alexandra told me, "There's no doubt that was the finest moment in our life together. Saul stood by me and helped in any way he could. Tried to protect me, to make it possible to visit my mother.

He was really wonderful. It was very tough on him; he wasn't used to doing this kind of thing." The Bucharest scenes of *The Dean* stay close to the facts. "He didn't actually have to invent anything," Alexandra remarked, "there was so much going on and it was all so dramatic and so brutal. He didn't exaggerate one iota. It was real life, told poetically by a great writer."

Romania takes up one half of *The Dean's December*; the other half is about Chicago. The 1980s was the winter of Bellow's own discontent with his home city. He was sometimes accused of squirreling himself away in Chicago—evidence that he must have had something to hide from the New York intellectual world. But what Bellow called his Chicago mood made him come back to the gray, sardonic, and coarse city, with its blunt-mannered men who had shoving cynicism written in their faces and who swore by an iron realism.

Chicago, dull and industrial, has always meant for many the wintry cramped reality of lives given up to hard, unforgiving work. For many more it was, and is, a bitter jail cell of poverty, crime, and chaos. By the early eighties, the time of *The Dean's December*, frozen-hell ghetto Chicago was bleeding over into wealthy white Chicago: when you walked around Hyde Park at night, you had best look over your shoulder; there were many neighborhoods whose red lights it would have been unwise to stop at; and even Lakeshore millionaires were not immune to mugging. It is this Chicago, looking like Dante's Dis transplanted to the Midwest, that Bellow describes in *The Dean*. The novel has a morgue atmosphere provided by its two cities, Chicago and Bucharest, both of them kingdoms of chill death, grimy and infernally cold. One of the book's scenes actually takes place in a morgue, where Bellow's hero identifies his mother-in-law's body.

Albert Corde, Bellow's hero, resembles a less imaginatively fertile Sammler. He is a balding middle-aged fellow, Scotch-Irish by heritage, and a Chicagoan of long vintage. His looks are aggressively plain; he is "a dish-faced man, long in the mouth." Bellow is experimenting here: never before did he feature a staid, stolid hero. A profound agitation is hidden inside Corde, but on the surface he shows not a ripple. Corde was a newspaperman for the *Paris Herald* before he entered academe. He is an outsider: a paltry white man to black Chicago, a fool to his university's provost, and a naïve American to his Romanian in-laws. Corde feels, Prufrock style, that he is "something of a stand-in, a journalist passing for a dean."

Corde is also, for once in Bellow, a nearly silent hero. "And now it seemed he had even forgotten how to open his mouth," Bellow writes. Like a James or Conrad protagonist, he is a reverberator. So is his wife, the famous astronomer who long ago left Romania for the West. Alexandra was the inspiration for both characters, Corde and Minna, both of them thoughtful, inward, and slow to ignite.

Yet the quiet Corde has his wild streak. "Corde had let himself go, indignant, cutting, reckless. He had made the college unhappy," Bellow writes. In the early pages of the novel, we learn that Corde has published two long articles in *Harper's* about the desperate state of inner city Chicago. (Bellow at the time had a nonfiction book contract for a volume on Chicago, which he never finished; he wrote *The Dean* instead.) Corde describes for his *Harper's* audience "the torments and wildness of black prisoners" in Cook County jail; the otherworldly shambles of a welfare hospital; and the frightening hell on earth of the Robert Taylor Homes, with their "young men getting on top of the elevator cabs, opening the hatch and threatening to pour in gas, to douse people with gasoline and set them afire."

Corde did something else along with his *Harper's* articles to stir the waters of university life: in his official role as dean, he involved himself in the Rick Lester case. Lester was a U. of C. student who was thrown through a window and killed during a robbery. Corde's own nephew, Mason, has been campaigning on behalf of the accused killer, a black man from the ghetto named Lucas Ebry.

Mason is a young radical "with a light, bright Huckleberry Finn air" and a calmly vicious streak, an air of "bright bitterness"; he resembles a shadowy figure of *ressentiment* out of Conrad. Bellow based Mason on Philip Grew, a nineteen-year-old U. of C. junior. Grew had threatened a witness who was ready to testify against his friend Ellis McInnis, his co-worker at an inner-city restaurant. In the summer of 1977 Ellis McInnis and Deola Johnson invaded the apartment of Mark and Crystal Gromer, tied up Mrs. Gromer, and threw her husband out the window when he tried to protect his wife. Mark Gromer was twenty-four, a graduate student in English at Chicago. His wife survived the ordeal. In *The Dean's December* Bellow turns Gromer into Rick Lester and Crystal into Lester's wife, whose suffering Bellow describes with tender respect.

The Dean directs itself to the filthy incorrigible facts of life in Chicago and Romania, but the book is also oriented toward the stars. It is Minna, with her farsighted astronomer's stance, who possesses the badly needed upward metaphysical angle. About Minna, Corde says, "She preferred looking up, definitely": "Why should slums, guns, drugs, jails, politics, intrigues, disorders matter? Leaving Hell, Dante saw the stars again. Minna saw them all the time." When she looks up, Minna also looks away from the urban inferno that troubles her husband. But Bellow insists that we remember both Minna's ethereal gaze and the irredeemable sorrows of black Chicago.

The Dean makes sure we cannot forget the hell of Chicago's ghettos. The black underclass, Corde sees, has been written off—doomed. We do not know how to attach them to life, because we ourselves, he argues, are not sufficiently attached either. The deeper question, Corde realizes, is "the slums we carry around inside us": Bellow tries in this phrase to forge a tie between his well-educated, mostly white audience and the deprivations he chronicles in *The Dean*. These black men and women are not aliens, he is saying, but our kindred who have been denied, turned away at society's gates. And no one knows how to welcome them in.

The terrible case of a rapist and murderer named Spofford Mitchell obsesses Corde. Mitchell is closely based on the real-life Hernando Williams. In 1978 Williams, the son of an African American minister, kidnapped a woman named Linda Goldstone, raped her, and locked her in the trunk of his car. He actually showed up to a court hearing for a previous rape and kidnapping with the victim still in his trunk. (People in the parking lot talked to Goldstone through the trunk lid and gave the car's license plate number to the police, but the police did nothing.) After Williams left the courtroom, still free on bail for his earlier crime, he raped Goldstone repeatedly and then killed her. The jury took less than an hour to decide on the death penalty for Williams.

In the novel, Corde discusses the murderer's case with Mitchell's public defender, who coolly fails to see the true horror of it. The conversation with the public defender, which appears in one of Corde's *Harper's* articles, contains Corde's own intense diagnosis of the problem. He says of Mitchell that "the man himself is filled with a staggering passion to break *through*," but can conceive only "the literalness of bodies and their members." When the woman begged for her life, what did he hear, what did he see? Corde wonders. The evil is in us, too, not just the murderer. "Our conception of physical life and of pleasure is completely death-saturated," Corde thinks. "The full physical emphasis is fatal. It cuts us off." Corde eloquently defends the murderer's victim against Mitchell's lawyer, who suggests she may have gone with Mitchell willingly.

The Dean is a book about character. Corde thinks of Valeria, Minna's mother, "with extraordinary respect," because "her humanity came from the old sources." In the hospital room that he and Minna have finally been allowed to visit, he leans close to her face and in a low voice impulsively tells her, "I also love you, Valeria." At this she becomes highly agitated, her face spasms and the monitors go wild. Valeria, Corde thinks, knows the truth of what he says. In *Ravelstein*, written after Bellow's divorce from Alexandra, the Romanian mother-in-law is far less sympathetic: the fact of having a Jewish son-in-law had poisoned her old age, decides Chick, *Ravelstein*'s narrator.

Valeria, all of her, will be consumed by death. After he sees her corpse in the hospital's morgue, Corde imagines her cremation. "At this very instant Valeria might be going into the fire," Corde thinks, "the roaring furnace which took off her hair, the silk scarf, grabbed away the green suit, melted the chased silver buttons, consumed the skin, flashed away the fat, blew up the organs, reached the bones, bore down on the skull—that refining fire, a ball of raging gold, a tiny sun, a star." The mystery of a human being's physical presence here takes on metaphysical coloring: behold the luminous center that so absurdly is just a material thing. In the end we will all be so reduced. Fired to a few pounds of hot ash, Valeria becomes mere matter, a little collapsed star.

The Dean's December favors subdued, reliable characters, and—unusually for Bellow—flamboyance comes in for serious knocks. One of the book's showy and false men is Corde's lawyer cousin Maxie (derived from Bellow's high school friend Sam Freifeld), who defends Lucas Ebry in court: "flashy, elderly, corrupt Maxie, with his bold eyes and his illiterate, furiously repetitious eloquence," who to impress women on the dance floor swings "his wide buttocks with crazy grace," his "massive, ecstatic face" like a Rouault.

Two stalwart black men uphold Bellow's book: Rufus Ridpath, a warden who tries to improve conditions at the county jail, and Toby Winthrop, an ex-hit man and drug addict who opens a community center in the ghetto. Another character describes Ridpath as "a plain kind of a man. He goes for duty"— the Conrad note again.

Bellow's two African American heroes are men of plain words and plain deeds. Winthrop physically demonstrates for Corde the work of his Operation Contact, leaning down to the floor and scooping upward with a powerful hand: "We reach for them and try to get a hold," he says. Mostly, he adds, his recovery center doesn't succeed, but there are always a few who can be saved. Once again, Bellow channels Conrad: it's the idea of the thing you must be loyal to, not the poor practical results. If Elya was the figure of duty in *Mr. Sammler's Planet*, here it is Winthrop, a man who tries desperately to prevent poor black America from being "written off"—words that Bellow also used to describe the fate of the European Jews in the 1930s and '40s. "His feeling for his people is real," Bellow writes of Ridpath. "Are they part of American society, or are they going to be eliminated from it?" More than thirty years later, Bellow's words still stand as a warning. Even though he was often typed as a conservative—and there is something conservative about the loyalty to duty that he champions in *The Dean's December*, and about his pessimism, too—Bellow's concern for what black America has to suffer is genuine.

The Dean is a sparse and unsparing book, its style deliberately matte, with no exuberance anywhere. Chicago looks like "a dirty snow brocade over the empty lots, and black men keeping warm at oil-drum bonfires," Bellow writes. But the novel has its metaphysics, too, with Bellow in an urgent downcast mood, whetted for philosophy. When Corde watches a class of black schoolchildren listening to *Macbeth* ("pity like a naked new-born babe, Striding the blast"), "restlessness stopped," he says. Corde, like the children, waits for an answer, but none exists. And so Bellow speaks quietly of *lacrimae rerum*, of love and mortality warring it out. Corde ruminates aloud to Minna's friend Vlada, "Tears may be intellectual, but they can never be political. They save no man from being shot, no child from being thrown alive into the furnace." These words are the credo of *The Dean*, which moves into Ivan Karamazov territory with the image of the dead child. Our tears of protest come from a whole heart and a whole mind, but they do not alter the world. Corde is a good man who cannot make life win out over death.

Bellow leaves us with the spare Cather-like epiphany of his conclusion, bringing us back to Alexandra, the upward-directed thinker in love with the stars. For her, truth is beauty. Corde gazes into the night sky above Palomar Observatory, where Minna has taken him to observe the sky. "This Mount Palomar coldness was not to be compared to the cold of the death house," Corde thinks. "Here the living heavens looked as if they would take you in." Such a fade-out into some far-off yet real depth, represented by Minna's astronomy, always lures Corde. The deep feeling between Corde and Minna—Bellow and Alexandra—generates the novel. Alexandra, like Minna, devotes herself to an abstract realm. But she needs Bellow, as Minna needs Corde. After the death of her mother, "what came through Minna's words was that she was alone in the world; and with him; she did have him, with all his troubling oddities; and he had her." Bellow here sounds, unusually, like James.

In *The Dean* Bellow gives us an unusually stripped-down, even slightly desolate, portrait of a loving relationship, with no marital hysterics, no crazy drama—no *Herzog*-like stunt work. Years earlier Bellow was Herzog; now he aspired to be Corde. The ambition was honorable, but in the end this was an impossible role for Bellow, with his wary, excitable sensibility. He needed a more provoking energy than Alexandra could give him. A crucial character was missing from *The Dean*'s severe landscapes: the comic, stormy iconoclast Allan Bloom, who would be the subject of Bellow's last book, *Ravelstein*.

CHAPTER 8

Allan Bloom

AFTER *The Dean's December* it would be almost twenty years before Bellow produced another major novel. (*More Die of Heartbreak*, which he published in 1987, is a minor book, and something of a rush job: Bellow wrote it in six months.) During much of this time he was teaching classes at Chicago with his raucous, charismatic friend Allan Bloom. Bloom was Bellow's new best friend on the Committee on Social Thought, his replacement for Shils. The passionate Bloom was the antithesis to Shils: unbuckled, hilarious, and greedy for life in the moment. Bloom would become Abe Ravelstein, a world-hungry intellectual who couldn't be more different from the straitlaced Artur Sammler.

The classes that Bloom and Bellow taught together usually focused on Stendhal, Flaubert, Conrad, Dostoevsky: Bellow's pantheon. Bloom had been a student of the hugely influential emigré political philosopher Leo Strauss, and like Strauss he became a cult figure among his students. He had the verve of a tummler and vaudevillian, he shared Bellow's ingrained suspicion of the intellectual establishment, and he was the kind of insatiable, never-resting personality that Bellow had always been drawn to. At the very end of the twentieth century, Bellow's last novel resurrects the emphatic, ravenous Jewish intellectual in a more achieved form than ever before in his work. Ravelstein is Humboldt and Zetland perfected. Bloom/Ravelstein thankfully lacks the madness that had afflicted Delmore Schwartz and, unlike Isaac Rosenfeld, he died only after he had had his vision, made his mark on the world.

Bloom, who was in all likelihood HIV-positive, fell ill with Guillain-Barré syndrome in 1990 and died in 1992. Bellow was by his bedside every day during his final months. Bloom wanted Bellow to tell his story, warts and all. Not until three years after Bloom's death did Bellow begin writing *Ravelstein*, his passionate homage to him. Bloom's ideas jibed with much of what Bellow had been thinking, though Bellow—unlike Bloom—didn't look for answers in the Greek classics. "Athens and Jerusalem is not my dish," Bellow wrote in *Ravelstein*.

To grasp the labor of love that is *Ravelstein*, and to see how Bellow ennobled Bloom in his last novel, we must read *Ravelstein* together with Bloom's own version of himself. In *The Closing of the American Mind*, Bloom wrote that from the moment he arrived at the University of Chicago as a teenager, "it seemed plausible to spend all my time thinking about what I am, a theme that was interesting to me but had never appeared a proper or possible subject of study." When he became a professor, Bloom passed this same high self-concern on to his students. Studying what you are, what you value, and then what you should value, forces you away from the easy pieties that you drank in from your parents and your hometown friends, before you met Bloom and started reading Thucydides, Plato, and the rest. Bellow in *Ravelstein* thinks hard about what Bloom was: a man who had gone far from his working-class Jewish roots to encounter ancient Greek wisdom, but who in his last days was more concerned with Jewishness than with any other topic.

Largely as a result of Bellow's urging, Bloom had become an influential figure in America. Bellow had for some time been prodding Bloom to write a book for a general audience, and sent Bloom to his agent, Harriet Wasserman. Bloom's commentaries on Plato and Rousseau were intricate scholarly contraptions, but he was learning to write more accessibly. *The Closing of the American Mind* became a best seller, and not just in America. Bloom's book was an opening salvo in the Culture Wars, and got him invitations from Ronald Reagan and Margaret Thatcher to discuss his ideas. Bloom did in Chicago what Trilling, Howe, and the others couldn't do in New York, stir a wide audience with his call to intellectual arms. He asked some basic questions: What kinds of people are needed in a liberal democracy like the United States? How can independence of thought be protected? In his book Bloom lambasted the America of the eighties, drenched, as he saw it, with too-easy formulas for personal fulfillment. He traced the American mania for self-seeking back to Nietzsche, who had spoken of creating one's own values. But America, Bloom said, had diluted the Nietzschean vision and toned it down, proclaiming that you had to choose the values that were right for you, rather than searching strenuously for the true ones. Relativism reigned, and in it Bloom detected a facile nihilism that was afraid to seek truth.

Officially, Bloom was a Platonist. But the secret hero of *The Closing of the American Mind* is Nietzsche—the real Nietzsche, not the limp American version. Bloom powerfully summarized Nietzsche's program: "In the present exhaustion of the old values, men must be brought to the abyss, terrified by their danger and nauseated by what could become of them. . . . Chaos, the war of opposites, is, as we know from the Bible, the condition of creativity, which must be mastered by the creator. The self must also bring forth arrows out of its longing." Like Nietzsche, Bloom despised the "peace virtuosos" determined to reduce conflict, the "skilled bow unbenders" who want us to adjust ourselves to reality.

Bloom was also, in his best seller, a follower of Thomas Mann. In Mann's *Death in Venice*, Bloom writes, Aschenbach's desires

> are somehow premonitory and like cries of the damned plunging into nothingness. Such desires search for significance—perhaps this is the case with everything erotic—but nothing in the world can

> give it to them. These desires are certainly not satisfied with the transfer of their cases from the tribunal of the judge and the priest to that of the doctor, or with being explained away. People can readily accept reductionism in everything except what most concerns them.

Bloom's paragraph on Mann, like his description of Nietzsche, has a taut personal intensity lacking from his mentions of Plato. The tolerance of sex that had come into fashion since the sixties was a cheapening of desire, Bloom writes, a reduction of eros to itching and scratching (Plato's pejorative image in the *Gorgias*). By contrast Mann hymns eros: its glory, its piercing independence from all social use and respectability. Bloom was, more than anything, a romantic solipsist who championed erotic and spiritual torment. Bellow, when he turned Bloom into Ravelstein, would change that. He transformed Bloom into a *shadchen* or matchmaker, an apostle of love and friendship. Gone was the severe Nietzschean Bloom of his best-selling book. In his place was Ravelstein with his intense sociability, which provides something that Alexandra, called Vela in the novel, is supposed to lack: a loving curiosity about other people.

Bellow's Ravelstein is at once an intellectual and a man of the people. Addicted to gossip, he watches the Chicago Bulls with his students. He wears expensive designer suits, which he ruins with coffee spills. Ravelstein is at heart a big kid who wants to rule the world: he stuffs himself on lime half-moon candies, studies Plato at all hours, and sends his students to work in the State Department. He rebels against the hidebound ideologists of the academy, since he holds to a higher idea of education. Ravelstein thrives on passionate involvement, and feels no need to hold back. His is a charmed life.

And so Bellow's writing is charmed too, in this, his final book. Bellow's style reaches in *Ravelstein* a high pitch of the art-that-conceals-art. His sentences wheel in circles as they try to encompass Ravelstein. Bellow's paragraphing in the novel becomes an art in itself, wielded like the supersharp pizza cutter that the "handsome Chinese prince" Nikki, Ravelstein's companion (based on Michael Wu, Bloom's boyfriend), uses to slice the pies delivered for the Chicago Bulls games that Ravelstein watches with his grad students. The loose sonatalike pattern of Bellow's book lets him downplay the majesty of his concern with the dead man. Many key scenes and even some sentences come back around in the text with musical variation. *Didn't he already talk about that?* the reader asks the author at first, and then realizes that the repetitions are deliberate. Memories of the loved friend recur: Bellow thinks about the fabulous creature Ravelstein and his death in a way that is neither brooding nor melancholy but instead becomes more lively with each recapitulation. Like all superb teachers, Ravelstein has his greatest hits, the lines he loves to say, the points he was born to make. Bellow echoes him by returning from time to time to his own favorite angles, his best sights of Ravelstein.

Ravelstein, the book and the man, is loaded with gossip.

But here gossip becomes a way to get at the enigma of a person. Even disreputable details should be worn with pride, Ravelstein suggests— "it's not gossip, it's social history," he jokes. The novel sketches barely veiled portraits of many of the friends and ex-friends of Bloom and Bellow: Edward Shils, Mircea Eliade, Paul Wolfowitz, Werner Dannhauser. Just as Alexandra, Bellow's ex-wife, becomes Vela, so does Janis Freedman, his new wife, become Rosamund. Rosamund is the ex-student of Ravelstein now married to Chick, Bellow's narrator. Rosamund's knowledge, like Ravelstein's, is on the side of life—she even revives Chick from near death. (Bellow had gone into a coma after eating poisoned fish on a 1994 trip he took to Saint Martin with Janis, an episode retold in the novel.)

Vela by contrast is the chilly scientist, alienated from personality and therefore from love. Alexandra asked Bellow for a divorce in 1985, the same year both his brothers died. Writing about the event more than ten years later, Bellow, it is clear, has not forgiven Alexandra. In his account she drifted silently, implacably away at the worst possible moment, just when his brothers had gone from him. Alexandra's own version is different. "He needed to renew himself," she said. "He needed new sources of inspiration. Toward the end of our marriage he would say, 'Look, she locks herself up in her study, I don't hear from her all morning, she doesn't care about me'—but that's the way things were from the very beginning, when he took great pride in me. He needed change, the old muse had to be deposed, and the new muse was waiting in the wings to be installed and anointed. So that was the natural process of things, I think now, in retrospect, but at the time I was very bewildered." The new muse was Janis, a woman forty-four years Bellow's junior.

Earlier, while their marriage was faltering, he had written to Maggie Staats criticizing Alexandra: "Where a woman's warmest sympathies should be there is a gap, something extracted in the earliest years of life which now is not even felt, not recognized as absent." Leon Wieseltier has a different take on Bellow and Alexandra. "He couldn't squash her," Wieseltier commented in our interview, adding, "the first one either" (referring to Anita, Bellow's first wife). Sondra and Susan had been awed by Bellow's creativity. But Alexandra lived in her own world, happily adjacent to her husband's but in many respects utterly unaffected by him. Knowing no math, Bellow could not share her deepest thinking. She remained strong and apart.

Bloom was the opposite of Alexandra: his high-pitched energy battled against her calm and reserved nature. The two became rivals. Bellow liked to have dinner with Bloom several times a week, and so Alexandra accused Saul of having an affair with him, a charge repeated, and rebutted, in *Ravelstein*. There was no affair, but as the marriage waned, Bloom became, more than Alexandra, Bellow's destined partner.

Yet Bloom had something in common with Alexandra: he too directed his thought upward toward heavenly patterns, Plato's ideas. Bellow in contrast was always a realist. Yet as he grew older he needed an interlocutor to instruct him in ideals, someone with a cosmic perspective on things. He wanted to test his novelist's realism against its opposite, whether it was Steiner's metaphysics, Alexandra's mathematics, or Bloom's political philosophy. Bellow had never before Alexandra known a living example of the pure idealist, someone devoted to the forms. Bloom too loved the forms, though his metaphysics was blended with lust: his trips to Paris, it was rumored, were filled with not just high culture but boys.

The final movement of *Ravelstein* centers on Jewishness, a subject that increasingly preoccupied Bellow in his final years. Jewishness was real but also metaphysical, since it was ideas and not worldly power that enabled the Jews to thrive. Ravelstein and Chick—Bloom and Bellow—agree that "it is impossible to get rid of one's origins, it is impossible not to remain a Jew." In his last days Ravelstein speaks often of Jews, and especially the Shoah. This in spite of the fact that Ravelstein has fled from his family and tried to become, in some basic soul sense, an ancient Greek.

"'The war made it clear that most people thought that almost everybody agreed that the Jews had no right to live," Chick remarks, adding, "That goes straight to your bones." The Jews "had lost the right to exist and were told as much by their executioners—'There is no reason why you should not die.'" What does it mean to the Jews that "so many others, millions of others, willed their death"? Chick and Ravelstein circle around this highly painful question. The Jews were chosen by the twentieth century, they conclude. The immense rage felt by so many at their mere existence, and the satisfaction and relief felt when Jews began to disappear, shows the darkest side of recent history. Chick says to Rosamund that in the twentieth century "there was a general willingness to live with the destruction of millions," in the Gulags, the labor camps. "It was like the mood of the century to accept it."

In Bellow's novel, the Holocaust continues to echo forty years later in Chicago. Ravelstein is concerned by the friendship that the eminent professor Radu Grielescu, Vela's fellow Romanian, has shown to Chick and Vela. Grielescu is drawn from Mircea Eliade, the courteous polymath scholar who enchanted generations of students with his wide-ranging reflections on myth, and who was close friends with Alexandra. Eliade in his youth had been a promoter of the viciously anti-Semitic Iron Guard. Ravelstein reminds Chick that Grielescu had supported the Guard, the "sadists who hung living Jews on meat hooks." In 1939 Eliade wrote, "The Poles' resistance in Warsaw is Jewish resistance. Only yids are capable of blackmail by putting women and children in the front line." Ravelstein, for his part, offers a piece of advice to Chick: "Just give a thought now and then to those people on the meat hooks."

Like *Herzog*, *Ravelstein* travels back to Bellow's childhood. In the middle of the book Bellow plants a loving quarrel between Chick and Ravelstein about Chick's "private metaphysics," his deep attachment to the pictures of the world that he saw as a little boy in Montreal. Before birth, "I had waited for millennia to see this," Bellow writes (a notion from the Russian thinker Vasily Rozanov). "Then when I had learned to walk—in the kitchen—I was sent down into the street to inspect it more closely":

> On Roy Street in Montreal a dray horse has fallen down on the icy pavement. . . . The long-haired Percheron with startled eyes and staring veins will need a giant to save him, but on the corner a crowd of small men can only call out suggestions. . . . Then there is a strange and endless procession of schoolgirls marching by twos in black uniform dresses. Their faces white enough to be tubercular. The nuns who oversee them keep their hands warm within their sleeves. The puddles in this dirt street are deep and carry a skim of ice.

Bellow had remembered the fallen horse half a century before, in his first novel, *Dangling Man*. Now he has come full circle. We see again Bellow's fierce attachment to his childhood memories, which appear in his work as pure and transparent as in Wordsworth's. This is his one turn to live, he says, to see, hear, and touch.

Ravelstein argues against Chick's private metaphysics. He says that "mankind [has] first claim on our attention," that we should pursue the pressing questions of truth and value, and avoid purely personal memories. But Chick, and Bellow, win the argument, and the proof is in *Ravelstein* itself, with its unparalleled portrait of a personality, Abe Ravelstein, who is in love not just with ideas but with people. Chick's early fledgling perceptions become in time a desire for the others who move close to you, letting you see their wrinkles, falterings, and strengths. Abe is just as drawn by people as Chick. Ravelstein quotes a Russian proverb, "the soul of another is a dark forest," and he plunges into that forest more often than he turns toward the Platonic sun.

After Ravelstein's death, while Chick and Rosamund are on their Caribbean vacation, Chick realizes that before he too dies he must finish his book about Ravelstein: "As Rosamund in her lovely voice sang 'Live-for-ever,' I thought of Ravelstein in his grave, all his gifts, his endlessly diverting character, and his intellect entirely motionless." Neither Chick nor Abe will live forever, none of us will, but, thanks to Chick, Abe's personal stamp will survive.

Bellow's writing becomes a way to make Bloom's charismatic personality live on, and to convince us he was a man who responded fully to others, someone who, like Bellow himself, led you to discover the true heft of people—not ideas, but people. (Of course, Bellow has turned Bloom into Ravelstein; the actual Bloom might have been less responsive, and less of a mensch, but it is the man in the novel who matters.) Bellow, revising Plato's myth of the cave, and alluding to the title of Bloom's *The Closing of the American Mind*, sees Bloom as his true other half:

> Since we are so often called upon for judgments, we naturally coarsen them by constant use or abuse. Then of course you see nothing original, nothing new; you are, in the end, no longer moved by any

> face, or any person. This is where Ravelstein had come in. He turned your face again toward the original. He forced you to reopen what you had closed.

"This is where Ravelstein had come in": a phrase from old-time movie houses, where spectators routinely entered after the picture had started. (Hollywood movies were, sometimes still are, designed to make sense to such latecomers.) This is where I came in, says Ravelstein, as he turns you toward the light.

Ravelstein is the perfect ending to Bellow's life of writing. Bellow's unexpected kind of literary revolution gravitates to the intimate and the gossipy, the life unraveled in faces and postures and loose talk. He goes in the opposite direction from high modernism, which too often sank the individual in grand ideas about culture, history, and society. Bellow also goes against the sense that we can make ourselves up freely, the facile low-rent Nietzscheanism that Bloom derided.

The way of writing that Bellow perfected was disarmingly personal. He let life invade his novels in a way matched by none of his contemporaries. Bellow is our biggest celebrator of personalities in all their strange, needy too-muchness. He had a deeply contrarian agenda, one we need now more than ever. The world is always telling us to invent a self, to become the person we want to be, to play a new role, or to savor a new twist of culture. Bellow tells us something else: we always are what we always were, body and soul. He opens us up, and we see.

ACKNOWLEDGMENTS

For sharing their memories of Saul Bellow with me and giving me generous permission to draw on them in this book, I would like to thank Max Apple, Adam Bellow, Daniel Bellow, Alexandra Ionescu Tulcea Bellow, Jonathan Brent, Stanley Crouch, Maggie Staats Simmons, Joan Ullman, and Leon Wieseltier. I also want to thank my hosts at the University of Chicago's Committee on Social Thought in May 2015, when I presented a talk drawn from this book: Rosanna Warren, Robert Pippin, Nathan Tarcov, and David Wellbery. Their comments have improved the book substantially. The special collections division of the Regenstein Library at the University of Chicago kindly assisted me during my consultation of the Saul Bellow, Isaac Rosenfeld, and Tarcov family collections.

My editor, Matt Weiland, and his assistant, Sam MacLaughlin, at Norton have been a tremendous help with the writing of this book; I am grateful for their hard work and their insight. Thanks go as well to Laura Goldin and Remy Cawley at Norton, to David LaRocca for help with the notes, and to Trent Duffy for copyediting. My agent, Chris Calhoun, deserves special thanks for his belief in this project.

In this book I have relied extensively on four essential earlier volumes: James Atlas's *Bellow*, Benjamin Taylor's *Saul Bellow: Letters* and his edition of Bellow's essays, *There Is Simply Too Much to Think About*, and Zachary Leader's *To Fame and Fortune: The Life of Saul Bellow, 1915–1964*. Ben Taylor and Zach Leader have shared their knowledge of Saul Bellow with me both informally and at a panel held at Columbia University in the fall of 2015; I wish to thank the organizer of that panel, Ross Posnock. My editors at *Tablet* magazine, David Samuels and Matthew Fishbane, and at the *Nation*, John Palatella, and at the *Yale Review*, J. D. McClatchy, gave me the chance to write about Bellow, for which I am also grateful. All three publications have given kind permission to reprint passages from these pieces in *Bellow's People*.

The Houstoun Endowment at the University of Houston helped pay for permissions costs, as did the Dean's Office of the College of Liberal Arts and Social Sciences.

NOTES

Quotations from Saul Bellow's novels are taken from the Library of America editions, *Novels 1944–1953*, *Novels 1956–1964*, and *Novels 1970–1982*, edited by James Wood, and from *Ravelstein* (New York: Viking, 2000).

The following abbreviations are used throughout the notes that follow.

Letters	Benjamin Taylor, ed., *Saul Bellow: Letters,* (New York: Viking, 2010)
Life of SB	Zachary Leader, *The Life of Saul Bellow: To Fame and Fortune, 1915–1964* (New York: Alfred A. Knopf, 2015)
There Is Simply	Saul Bellow, *There Is Simply Too Much to Think About* (New York: Viking, 2015)

INTRODUCTION

11 "He was going to take on": Alfred Kazin, *New York Jew* (New York: Alfred A. Knopf, 1978).

12 "Instantly we know": Ralph Waldo Emerson, *The American Scholar* (1837).

13 In Bellow's descriptions: James Wood in *The Irresponsible Self* (New York: Picador, 2004).

15 "expansive, toothy smile": Joseph Epstein, "Another Rare Visit with Noah Danzig," *Commentary* (October 1990).

16 "He brought Harold back": Interview with Joan Ullman.

17 "self-alienation, historical dislocation": Jonathan Liu, review of Joshua Cohen's *Witz* in *Barnes and Noble Review* (June 3, 2010).

18 "to memorize most of Genesis": SB, "A Jewish Writer in America" (2011), in *There is Simply.*

19 "I would call the attitudes": SB, introduction to *Great Jewish Short Stories* (New York: Dell, 1963), reprinted in *There Is Simply.*

19 Fiedler issued a call to arms: Leslie Fiedler, "What Can We Do About Fagin?" *Commentary* (May 1949) and "The Jewish Writer and the English Literary Tradition: A Symposium (Parts I and II)," *Commentary* (September and October, 1949).

19 "prayer shawls and phylacteries": SB, introduction, *Great Jewish Short Stories.*

20 "The real secret": Ibid.

20 "'I have suffered'": Susan Cheever, *Note Found in a Bottle* (New York: Simon and Schuster, 1999).

20 "Things around Saul": Interview with Leon Wieseltier.

21 "I don't consider myself": SB to Leslie Fiedler, June 14, 1955, in *Letters.*

21 "A cold coming": SB to Anne Sexton, n.d., in *Letters.*

22 "once told me that": Interview with Adam Bellow.

22 "The individual in American fiction": SB, "Some Notes on Recent American Fiction" (1963), in *There Is Simply.*

27 "He reminded many people": Edward Rothstein, "Saul Bellow, Saul Bellow, Let Down Your Hair," *New York Times* (April 9, 2005).

28 "At a most susceptible time": SB interview with Chirantan Kulshrestha (1972), in *Conversations with Saul Bellow*, ed. Gloria L. Cronin and Ben Siegel (Oxford: University of Mississippi Press, 1994).

28 "I went across the street": SB interview with Norman Manea, in Manea, *Saul Bellow: Settling My Accounts Before I Go Away* (Rhinebeck, N.Y.: Sheep Meadow Press, 2013).

29 "in a state of high excitement": Irving Howe, *A Margin of Hope* (New York: Harcourt Brace Jovanovich, 1984).

29 *Az Got git pleytzes*: Isaac Bashevis Singer, *Gimpl Tam un andere Dertseylungen* (New York: CYCO, 1963).

29 "Shoulders are from God": "Gimpel the Fool," *Partisan Review* (May 1953).

30 "Sometimes he twinkles": SB, "The Swamp of Prosperity" (1959), in *There Is Simply*.

30 "charm was like a moat": Philip Roth, *The Ghost Writer* (New York: Farrar, Straus and Giroux, 1979).

31 "I loved the depiction": Interview with Adam Bellow.

31 "essay after essay": SB, "The Nobel Lecture" (1976), in *There Is Simply*.

CHAPTER 1: MORRIE BELLOWS

37 "My father, spongy soul": SB to Oscar Tarcov, 1937, Tarcov Family Collection, box 1, Regenstein Library, University of Chicago.

38 "Fuck Morrie": Interview with Adam Bellow.

38 "He terrified me": Interview with Daniel Bellow.

39 "ran to the partner's": Quoted in *Life of SB*.

39 "a furious man": SB to Irving Halperin, n.d., quoted in ibid.

40 "Enough of this crap": Morrie Bellows, quoted in ibid.
40 "freezes when he's offended": SB to Susan Glassman, January 1962, in *Letters*.
41 "He liked to abuse waiters": Greg Bellow, quoted in *Life of SB*.
41 "Who's this guy Prowst?": Morrie Bellows's remark remembered by his daughter, Lynn Rotblatt, quoted in ibid.
42 "He sees none of us": SB to Dean Borok, June 17, 1980, in *Letters*.
43 "You *never* looked this good": Dean Borok to SB, 1992, quoted in *Life of SB*.
45 "He overpowered me": SB interview with Philip Roth (1998–2000), in *There Is Simply*.
46 "The boldest comedians": SB, "Wit Irony Fun Games" (2003), in ibid.
47 "He was focused": Dave Peltz, quoted in *Life of SB*.
49 "speculative biography": SB interview with Roth.
49 "wild time . . . stirred to the depths": SB interview with Maggie Simmons (1979), in *Conversations with Saul Bellow*, ed. Gloria L. Cronin and Ben Siegel (Oxford: University of Mississippi Press, 1994).
49 "In American literature": Irving Howe, "Strangers," *Yale Review* (June 1977).
50 "the 'good' writing": SB, "Dreiser and the Triumph of Art," in *There Is Simply*.
51 "Augie reminds us": Norman Podhoretz, review of *The Adventures of Augie March*, *Commentary* (October 1953).
51 "American Jewish style": Howe, "Strangers."
57 "You seem to have accepted": SB to Philip Roth, January 7, 1984, in *Letters*.
57 a girl really named Fenchel: Raysh Weiss, personal communication.

60 "It's Saul's gift": Lionel Trilling to Pascal Covici, 1953, quoted in James Atlas, *Bellow* (New York: Random House, 2000).

60 "I made many mistakes": SB to Bernard Malamud, n.d., in *Letters*.

61 "disappointment with its human material": SB, "The Sealed Treasure" (1960), in *There Is Simply*.

61 "The book made a hit": Quoted in Atlas, *Bellow*. Leader gives a slightly different version of the letter (Atlas has corrected Abraham's spelling).

61 "It's just like my father": SB to Sam Freifeld, October 19, 1953, in *Letters*.

62 "A few years ago": SB to Sam Freifeld, November 30, 1953, in ibid.

CHAPTER 2: RALPH ELLISON

65 "You know I carry a knife": Quoted in Arnold Rampersad, *Ralph Ellison* (New York: Alfred A. Knopf, 2007).

66 "*Vos voln zey fun mir?*": Personal communication from Max Apple.

68 "It all began": Ralph Ellison, introduction to the thirtieth-anniversary edition of *Invisible Man*, in John Callahan, ed., *Collected Essays of Ralph Ellison* (New York: Random House, 1995).

69 "bent upon finding his way": Ibid.

71 "being my animal self": Norman Manea, *Saul Bellow: Settling My Accounts Before I Go Away* (Rhinebeck, N.Y.: Sheep Meadow Press, 2013).

73 "a superb book": SB, "Man Underground: On Ralph Ellison" (1952), in *There Is Simply*.

73 "having once a week sessions": Ralph Ellison and Albert Murray, *Trading Twelves* (New York: Modern Library, 2000).

74 "the first real novel": Quoted in Rampersad, *Ralph Ellison.*

76 "the epitome of Negro": Rampersad, *Ralph Ellison.*

77 "You cannot have an American experience": Ralph Ellison, "Alain Locke" (1974), in *Collected Essays.*

77 "*All* us old-fashioned": Ralph Ellison, "Indivisible Man" (1970), in *Collected Essays.*

77 "a black Jew": Quoted in ibid. (the 1969 panel discussion occurred at Brown University).

78 "The World and the Jug" can be found in Ellison's *Collected Essays*; Howe's "Black Boys and Native Sons" is in his *A World More Attractive* (New York: Horizon, 1963).

79 "and my husband would sit": Quoted in Rampersad, *Ralph Ellison.*

79 "beautiful": SB to Ruth Miller, July 27, 1955, in *Letters.*

82 "I could have gone out with Philip": Quoted in James Atlas, *Bellow* (New York: Random House, 2000).

83 "know which parts": SB to Ralph Ellison, n.d., in *Letters.*

83 "emptying his lungs": Quoted in Atlas, *Bellow.*

83 "I have yet to see": SB letter to Pascal Covici, n.d., in *Letters.*

83 "We've bought ourselves": SB to Ralph Ellison, 1956, in *Letters.*

84 "Bellowview": Quoted in Greg Bellow, *Saul Bellow's Heart* (New York: Bloomsbury, 2013).

84 "Look at my tomatoes": Rosette Lamont, "Bellow Observed: A Serial Portrait," *Saul Bellow Journal* (Summer 1985; originally published in *Mosaic*, 1974).

85 "*pays de merveilles*": SB to Theodore Weiss, n.d., in *Letters.*

85 "wear beards": Quoted in Rampersad, *Ralph Ellison.*

85 "Kiss me": Quoted in ibid.

85 "What's a jungle bunny": Quoted in ibid.

85 "Gore, I just don't understand": Interview with Daniel Bellow.

86 "I get a few hundred": SB to Ellison, n.d., in *Letters.*

86 "like a nineteenth century": Ellison, *Trading Twelves.*

86 "As writers are natural": SB, preface to Ellison, *Collected Essays.*

86 "a writer's block": Quoted in Rampersad, *Ralph Ellison.*

87 "encouraged Ralph": Quoted in ibid.

87 "powers of organization": Quoted in ibid.

87 "Ralph had the bearing": SB, preface to Ellison, *Collected Essays.*

88 "Ralph wouldn't let them give": Quoted in Rampersad, *Ralph Ellison.*

89 "the Negro stereotype": Ralph Ellison, "Twentieth-Century Fiction and the Black Mask of Humanity" (1953), in *Collected Essays.*

89 "He was always making and breaking families": Interview with Adam Bellow.

93 "schmaltzed-up": Philip Roth, interview with Joyce Carol Oates (1974), in *Conversations with Philip Roth*, ed. George Searles (Oxford: University of Mississippi, 1992).

94 "thrown millions of light years": SB to Gertrude Buckman, August 2 1956, in *Letters.*

94 "I think and think about Isaac": SB to John Berryman, December 1956, in ibid.

CHAPTER 3: ISAAC ROSENFELD AND CHANLER CHAPMAN

95 "Isaac had a round face": SB, foreword to Isaac Rosenfeld, *An Age of Enormity* (New York: World, 1962).

97 "the Chicago Dostoevskyans": Steven Zipperstein, *Rosenfeld's Lives* (New Haven: Yale University Press, 2009).

97 "emotional hunger incapable of being sated": Ibid.

98 "I will say to you": Isaac Rosenfeld to Oscar Tarcov, November 1941, Isaac Rosenfeld Collection, box 1, folder 10, Regenstein Library, University of Chicago.

98 "simper[ing] self-consciously": Isaac Rosenfeld, "The

Precious Student at the University of Chicago," *The Beacon* (1937).

98 "the renaissance of Isaac": SB to Oscar Tarcov, September 29, 1937, Tarcov Family Collection, box 1, Regenstein Library, University of Chicago.

98 "foaming rabbis rub electrical fish": Quoted in Zipperstein, *Rosenfeld's Lives*.

99 "An old Roman article of diet": Quoted in ibid.

99 "'Yet there lives the dearest freshness'": Isaac Rosenfeld, Journal 1955–1956, Rosenfeld Collection, box 3, folder 4, Regenstein Library.

99 "pagan beauty": Isaac Rosenfeld to Oscar Tarcov, n.d., Rosenfeld Collection, box 2, folder 1, ibid.

100 "I have been reading *Moby-Dick*": Isaac Rosenfeld to Oscar Tarcov, March 28, 1941, Rosenfeld Collection, box 1, folder 10, ibid.

101 "It was still a shame": David Bazelon, *Nothing but a Fine Tooth Comb* (New York: Simon and Schuster, 1970).

101 "Isaac was my friend": D. J. R. Bruckner, "A Candid Talk with Saul Bellow," *The New York Times Magazine* (April 15, 1984).

102 "became a fanatical Reichian": Ibid.

103 "kosher fry beef": Rosenfeld, "Adam and Eve on Delancey Street" (1949), in Isaac Rosenfeld, *Preserving the Hunger*, ed. Mark Shechner (Detroit: Wayne State University Press, 1988).

104 "air of yeshiva purity": Irving Howe quoted in Zipperstein, *Rosenfeld's Lives*.

104 "I feel much more alive": Isaac Rosenfeld to Oscar Tarcov, April 3, 1951, Rosenfeld Collection, box 1, folder 11, Regenstein Library.

104 "I feel 500,000 years older": Isaac Rosenfeld to Oscar

Tarcov, January 10, 1953, Rosenfeld Collection, box 1, folder 11, ibid.

104 "I have attacks of hatefulness": Rosenfeld notebooks (n.d.), Rosenfeld Collection, box 2, folder 11, ibid.

104 "It's awful, being alone in Chicago": Rosenfeld notebooks (1955), Rosenfeld Collection, box 1, folder 11, ibid.

105 "He died in a seedy, furnished room": SB, "On Isaac Rosenfeld," *Partisan Review* (Winter 1956). In this essay Bellow remarked, "The victories he wanted were those of the heart. Ecstasy was what he pursued, and he paid the cost in suffering, a horrible and bloody cost."

106 "I loved him, but we were rivals": SB, preface to Rosenfeld, *An Age of Enormity.*

106 "tired of being envied": SB to Oscar Tarcov, March 26, 1956, Tarcov Family Collection, box 1, Regenstein Library.

106 "Someday Saul": Isaac Rosenfeld to Monroe Engel, quoted in Zipperstein, *Rosenfeld's Lives.*

106 "It should have been Isaac": Ibid.

107 "There are times": SB to Henry Volkening, October 19, 1955, in *Letters.*

109 "I need it for some of the details": SB to Samuel Goldberg, n.d., in *Letters.*

113 "tragic or near-tragic": Daniel Middleton, "The Chanler Chapman Show," *About Town* (Dutchess County, N.Y.) (n.d.).

113 "Politics takes physique": John Jay Chapman, quoted in Edmund Wilson, "John Jay Chapman" (1937), in *The Triple Thinkers* (New York: Harcourt, Brace, 1938).

113 "The case was simple": Ibid.

114 "Who was this outrageous Ahab": Middleton, "The Chanler Chapman Show."

114 "a great big school": Chanler Chapman, *The Wrong Attitude* (New York: Putnam, 1940).

115 "He seemed to know": Middleton, "The Chanler Chapman Show."

115 "I never had a better time": Quoted in ibid.

115 "The two things I liked": Chanler Chapman, "Eight Days in a Lifeboat," *Life* magazine (September 28, 1942).

116 "Step in and enjoy": Chanler Chapman, quoted in Middleton, "The Chanler Chapman Show."

116 "I'm aware that it gets mixed up": SB to Josephine Herbst, August 15, 1959, in *Letters*.

116 "Every ability was brought": SB to Richard Stern, November 3, 1959, in ibid.

CHAPTER 4: SONDRA TSCHACBASOV AND JACK LUDWIG

118 "wallow[ed] with full art": John Berryman to SB, n.d., quoted in *Life of SB*.

122 "point-blank if I was sleeping with Saul yet": Sondra Tschacbasov quoted in ibid.

123 "What a relief from my whirling dervish": Ibid.

124 "A bulky Winnipeg hockey body": Keith Botsford quoted in *Life of SB*.

124 "butcher boy Yiddish": SB quoted in ibid.

124 "this very round faced": Sondra Tschacbasov quoted in ibid.

124 "Ludwig was very expansive": Ibid.

125 "Saul was disapproving": Ibid.

125 "He wanted to *be* Saul Bellow": quoted in *Life of SB*.

126 "A young girl requires": SB to John Berryman, n.d., in *Letters*.

126 "I looked into his eyes": Sondra Tschacbasov quoted in *Life of SB*.

126 "Sasha is an absolutist": SB to Keith Botsford, November 5, 1959, in *Letters*.

127 "sixteen hours a day": SB to Pascal Covici, October 2, 1958, in ibid.

127 "Boring subjects delight her": SB to Ralph Ellison, n.d., in ibid.

127 "She took the kid": SB to Josephine Herbst, January 31, 1959, in ibid.

127 "Sondra too is much better": SB to Pascal Covici, February 19, 1959, in ibid.

129 "I sometimes long for Adam": SB to Jonas Schwartz, October 19, 1960, in ibid.

129 "It was impossible to recognize": Interview with Adam Bellow.

130 "I have good grounds": SB to Pascal Covici, November 10, 1959, in *Letters.*

130 "old Tschacbasov . . . was a repulsive": SB to Stanley Elkin, July 22, 1992, in ibid.

130 "Anyway she walked into the living room": SB to Pascal Covici, November 1, 1959, in ibid.

131 pained by Brent's mistakes: Interview with Jonathan Brent.

133 "The profile is that of a witty": Rosette Lamont, "Bellow Observed: A Serial Portrait," *Saul Bellow Journal* (Summer 1985; originally published in *Mosaic,* 1974).

134 "wonderful sense of peace": Rosette Lamont, "The Confessions of Moses Herzog," *Massachusetts Review* (Spring–Summer 1965).

134 "If I hadn't gone off": SB to Marshall Best, March 16, 1960, in *Letters.*

135 "I haven't got the sharpest eyes": SB to Jack Ludwig. n.d., in ibid.

136 "siege of self-justification": Jack Ludwig, "The Wayward Reader," *Holiday* (February 1965).

136 "ingenious, shrewd, supersubtle": SB to Alfred Kazin, January 28, 1965, in *Letters.*

137 "The letters of the heroine": SB to Sondra Tschacbasov, n.d., in ibid.

137 "I threw one leg up": Jack Ludwig, *Above Ground* (New York: Little, Brown, 1968).

139 "The tragedies of my life": Sondra Tschacbasov quoted in *Life of SB*.

139 "Saul was hurt": Quoted in ibid.

140 "the depressed sense": SB to Susan Glassman, January 23, 1961, in *Letters*.

141 "He used to work up a sweat": Interview with Adam Bellow.

141 wonderful: Interview with Maggie Staats Simmons.

141 "I miss you so much": Maggie Staats to SB, April 5, 1966, in *Letters*.

142 "Unwillingness, reluctance to recognize": SB, journals (1966), quoted in James Atlas, *Bellow* (New York: Random House, 2000).

143 "He kept making and breaking families": Interview with Adam Bellow.

CHAPTER 5: EDWARD SHILS

145 "chump" and a "sentimentalist": SB to Philip Roth, January 1, 1998, in *Letters*.

146 "I love Edward": SB quoted in James Atlas, *Bellow* (New York: Random House, 2000).

146 "I refuse to let him use": Quoted in ibid.

146 "unlanced boil": Quoted in ibid.

146 "I have no wish": Quoted in ibid.

149 "How could one have any respect": Edward Shils, *A Fragment of a Sociological Autobiography* (New Brunswick, N.J.: Transaction, 2006).

149 "I thought they were rather foolish": Ibid.

150 "Do you know any intelligent": SB quoted in Joseph Epstein, "My Friend Edward," introduction to Edward Shils, *Portraits: A Gallery of Intellectuals* (Chicago: University of Chicago Press, 1997).

150 "did his homework": Interview with Alexandra Ionescu Tulcea Bellow.

150 "a pronunciation system": Epstein, "My Friend Edward."

150 "Joseph, note those three": Ibid.

151 "Mr. Fairlie, you wrote some": Ibid.

152 "he is a man who often laughs": Ibid.

153 "the emancipation of the individual": Edward Shils, "Totalitarians and Antinomians," in *Political Passages*, ed. John Bunzell (New York: Free Press, 1988).

154 "embracing the black students": Edward Shils, "The Political University and Academic Freedom," *Minerva* (October 1970).

155 Dostoevsky had taught him something: Interview with Stanley Crouch.

155 "the wisest artwork": John Berryman to his mother, n.d., quoted in Atlas, *Bellow.*

156 "*Sammler* isn't even a novel": SB to Daniel Fuchs, April 10, 1974, in *Letters.*

156 "Where that book has intellectual content": Norman Manea, *Saul Bellow: Settling My Accounts Before I Go Away* (Rhinebeck, N.Y.: Sheep Meadow Press, 2013).

159 "You're a fucking square": Quoted in Andrew Gordon, "*Mr. Sammler's Planet*," in *A Political Companion to Saul Bellow*, ed. Gloria L. Cronin and Lee Trepanier (Lexington: University Press of Kentucky, 2013).

159 "So I left the platform" . . . "denounced by Salas": SB to Mark Harris, October 22, 1968, in *Letters.*

161 "hip, which would return": Norman Mailer, "The White Negro," *Dissent* (Fall 1957).

162 “It is thought that Negroes”: SB, “Man Underground,” *Commentary* (June 1952), reprinted in *There Is Simply*.

162 “blacks, according to this view”: Edward Shils, “Learning and Liberalism,” in *The Selected Papers of Edward Shils*, vol. 3 (Chicago: University of Chicago Press, 1980).

164 “that superior Krautess”: SB to Leon Wieseltier, January 18, 1978, in *Letters*.

167 “liberals would sooner see”: Shils, “Totalitarians and Antinomians.”

CHAPTER 6: DELMORE SCHWARTZ

169 “The proud and regal”: Lou Reed, *The Blue Mask* (1982).

170 “Dwight [Macdonald] cheated”: John Berryman, *Dream Songs* (New York: Farrar, Straus and Giroux, 2014).

174 “the eye of a Mongol horseman”: Robert Lowell, “In Dreams Begin Responsibilities,” in *History* (New York: Farrar, Straus and Giroux, 1973).

175 “a development Delmore”: James Atlas, *Delmore Schwartz* (New York: Farrar, Straus and Giroux, 1977).

175 “Philip has scruples”: Quoted in ibid.

175 “Just before eating”: Delmore Schwartz, *Portrait of Delmore* (New York: Farrar, Straus and Giroux, 1986).

175 “curious hop”: William Barrett, *The Truants* (New York: Doubleday Anchor, 1983).

176 “my strange delightful buddy”: SB to Sam Freifeld, April 1954, in *Letters*.

176 “About Delmore”: SB to James Laughlin, October 22, 1957, in ibid.

182 “I watch her”: Quoted in James Atlas, *Bellow* (New York: Random House, 2000).

183 “the idea of art”: Manny Farber, “White Elephant Art vs. Termite Art” (1962), in *Farber on Film*, ed. Robert Polito (New York: Library of America, 2009).

184 "the continuity, harmony": Ibid.
185 "in which the hero": Delmore Schwartz and James Laughlin, *Selected Letters*, ed. Robert Phillips (New York: W. W. Norton, 1993).

CHAPTER 7: ALEXANDRA IONESCU TULCEA BELLOW

189 "Well, I haven't read": Interview with Alexandra Ionescu Tulcea Bellow.
191 "Yup, yup": Harriet Wasserman, *Handsome Is* (New York: Fromm, 1997).
191 "They had something": Dumitru Bagdasar, quoted in Alexandra Ionescu Tulcea Bellow, "Asclepios Versus Hades in Romania," *Revista 22* (August 23 and August 31, 2004).
191 "You could have had a penthouse": Quoted in ibid.
192 "Do you think Hades": Quoted in ibid.
192 "a princely personality": Ibid.
194 "A room thirteen floors": D. J. R. Bruckner, "A Candid Talk with Saul Bellow," *The New York Times Magazine* (April 15, 1984). According to Alexandra, she bought both apartments for the couple.
195 "It was loud as can be": Interview with Alexandra Ionescu Tulcea Bellow.
195 "You cannot believe how oblivious": Bruckner, "A Candid Talk with Saul Bellow."
196 "It was magical": Interview with Alexandra Ionescu Tulcea Bellow.
196 "How was Stockholm?" . . . "Meshuga!": Quoted in Wasserman, *Handsome Is*.
196 "I was drunk": Interview with Daniel Bellow.
197 "very dramatic": Interview with Alexandra Ionescu Tulcea Bellow.
198 "When the Russians": SB, *To Jerusalem and Back* (New York: Viking, 1976).

198 "There's no doubt": Interview with Alexandra Ionescu Tulcea Bellow.

CHAPTER 8: ALLAN BLOOM

210 "it seemed plausible": Allan Bloom, *The Closing of the American Mind* (New York: Simon and Schuster, 1987).

212 "In the present exhaustion": Ibid.

212 "are somehow premonitory": Ibid.

215 "He needed to renew": Interview with Alexandra Ionescu Tulcea Bellow.

216 "Where a woman's warmest sympathies": SB to Maggie Staats, September 16, 1984, in *Letters*.

216 "He couldn't squash her": Interview with Leon Wieseltier.

218 "The Poles' resistance": Mircea Eliade, quoted in Norman Manea, *The Fifth Impossibility* (New Haven: Yale University Press, 2012).

CREDITS

Excerpts from *The Adventures of Augie March* by Saul Bellow, copyright 1949, 1951, 1952, 1953, renewed © 1977, 1980, 1981 by Saul Bellow, used by permission of The Wiley Agency LLC and Viking Books, an imprint of Penguin Publishing Group, a division of Penguin Random House LLC.

Excerpts from *The Dean's December* by Saul Bellow, copyright © 1982 by Saul Bellow, used by permission of The Wylie Agency LLC.

Excerpts from *Herzog* by Saul Bellow, copyright © 1961, 1963, 1964, renewed 1989, 1991 by Saul Bellow, used by permission of Viking Books, an imprint of Penguin Publishing Group, a division of Penguin Random House LLC; from *Herzog* by Saul Bellow (Weidenfeld & Nicolson 1970, Penguin Books 1972, 1977, 2004, Penguin Classics 2007), copyright © Saul Bellow, 1969, 1970, reproduced by permission of Penguin Books Ltd.

Excerpts from *Humboldt's Gift* by Saul Bellow, copyright © 1973, 1974, 1975 by Saul Bellow, used by permission of Viking

Books, an imprint of Penguin Publishing Group, a division of Penguin Random House LLC, and The Wylie Agency LLC.

Excerpts from *Mr. Sammler's Planet* by Saul Bellow, copyright © 1969, 1970 by Saul Bellow, used by permission of The Wiley Agency LLC and Viking Books, an imprint of Penguin Publishing Group, a division of Penguin Random House LLC; from *Mr. Sammler's Planet* by Saul Bellow (Weidenfeld & Nicolson 1970, Penguin Books 1972, 1977, 2004, Penguin Classics 2007), copyright © Saul Bellow, 1969, 1970, reproduced by permission of Penguin Books Ltd.

Excerpts from *Ravelstein* by Saul Bellow, copyright © 2000 by Saul Bellow, used by permission of Viking Books, an imprint of Penguin Publishing Group, a division of Penguin Random House LLC; from *Ravelstein* by Saul Bellow (Penguin General, 2000), copyright © Saul Bellow, 2000, 2001, reproduced by permission of Penguin Books Ltd.

Excerpts from *Saul Bellow: Letters* by Saul Bellow, edited by Benjamin Taylor, copyright © 2010 by Janis Bellow. Used by permission of Viking Books, an imprint of Penguin Publishing Group, a division of Penguin Random House LLC.

Excerpts from *The Life of Saul Bellow* by Zachary Leader, copyright © 2015 by Zachary Leader, used by permission of Alfred A. Knopf, a division of Penguin Random House LLC.

Materials from the Regenstein Library's Isaac Rosenfeld Archive used courtesy of the Special Collections Research Center, University of Chicago Library.

INDEX